EAST DULWICH
remembered

Green & Blue wine shop and wine bar at No. 38 Lordship Lane now occupies premises previously used by Redgewell's butcher's shop and later by Woods. When the premises were taken over by Redgewell's Coffee Shop, Redgewell's old sign was found behind the one which had been put up by Woods.

EAST DULWICH

remembered

JOHN D. BEASLEY

AMBERLEY

Other local history books by John D. Beasley in print:

Building Together: The Story of Peckham Methodist Church
Peckham Methodist Church, Wood's Road, London SE15 2PX
Who Was Who in Peckham
Chener Books Ltd, 14 Lordship Lane, London SE22 8HN
The Bitter Cry Heard and Heeded:
The Story of the South London Mission of the Methodist Church 1889-1989
South London Mission, Central Hall, Bermondsey Street, London SE1 3UJ
Save Green Spaces from Destruction by Food Giants
Obtainable from South Riding Press
Transport in Peckham and Nunhead
South Riding Press, 6 Everthorpe Road, London SE15 4DA
East Dulwich: An Illustrated Alphabetical Guide
Chener Books
The Story of Peckham and Nunhead
Southwark Local History Library, 211 Borough High Street, London SE1 1JA
Peckham & Nunhead Through Time
East Dulwich Through Time
Camberwell Through Time
Origin of Place Names in Peckham and Nunhead
Amberley Publishing

This edition first published 2010

Amberley Publishing
Cirencester Road, Chalford,
Stroud, Gloucestershire, GL6 8PE
www.amberleybooks.com

British Library Cataloguing in Publication Data.
A catalogue record for this book is available from the British Library.

ISBN 978 1 4456 0138 0

Typesetting and Origination by Amberley Publishing.
Printed in Great Britain.

Contents

Introduction   6

Acknowledgements   10

1   Homes   11

2   Wartime   23

3   Education   36

4   Commerce   55

5   Parks and Public Services   72

6   Recreation   82

7   Places of Worship   101

8   Transport   114

Introduction

East Dulwich is a well preserved Victorian suburb now home to a growing number of affluent people who prefer to live close to the city rather than commute from Kent or Surrey.

Though I was born in Yorkshire and brought up in Lincolnshire, I have lived close to East Dulwich for thirty-eight years. Before numbered postal districts were introduced in 1917, the southern end of Peckham SE15, where I live close to Goose Green, was in East Dulwich.

Grove Vale and Lordship Lane are my 'village street' where the local shops provide a good friendly service by many people who have come from around the world to live and work in East Dulwich.

Writing *East Dulwich: An Illustrated Alphabetical Guide*, the first book exclusively on SE22, was an interesting and enriching experience. As a sequel, I enjoyed compiling the original version of *East Dulwich Remembered* which shed new light on SE22.

My own memories of living close to East Dulwich go back to 1972. Though St Francis Hospital was closed in 1991, in my front garden is a beautiful fuchsia which I bought from a fête at the hospital.

The jewel in the East Dulwich crown is undoubtedly Peckham Rye Park which many people do not realise is in SE22. On the radio during the centenary celebrations in 1994, I described it as the most beautiful park in the London Borough of Southwark. When I paid my second visit to Kazakhstan in the former Soviet Union, to do drug education work on behalf of Hope UK, I showed two school classes a photograph of a heron sitting on a branch in the Peckham Rye Park lake. The gasps of amazement from the pupils, who live in a city built in a desert, were the Russian equivalent of 'Wow!' Peckham Rye Park must never be taken for granted and we should be grateful to the Victorians who campaigned to convert Homestall Farm into a much needed park.

Though I enjoy playing cricket in Dulwich Park SE21, which is also beautiful, my highest score in cricket – 100 not out – was made on Goose Green where my son Michael also scored a century when he was fourteen.

Parks and other green spaces are vital for people's mental and physical health, particularly in inner city areas like East Dulwich. That is why the biggest campaign in this district was the one which tried to prevent Sainsbury's from destroying over eight acres of open green space so a store could be built at Dog Kennel Hill. The story of the action local people took to try to save King's College sports ground, and other land which had never been built on, is told in *Save Green Spaces From Destruction By Food Giants*. Thankfully, a major campaign prevented a Homebase store being built on Dulwich Hamlet Football Ground, which was opened on 3 October 1992. Yet another new Dulwich Hamlet Football Ground would have destroyed the ten acres of Green Dale playing fields which were open countryside when John Ruskin lived at nearby Denmark Hill in the nineteenth century.

Above: A street party was held in 1935 to celebrate the Silver Jubilee of King George V and Queen Mary. In the background can be seen Cook's grocer's shop in North Cross Road.

Right: Homestall Playing Fields are part of what used to be a much larger sports ground where Honor Oak Cricket Club played. On Sunday 13 June 1926, H. Eaitch (116) and T.A.C. Maxwell (217 not out) achieved a second wicket partnership of 300 against Highbury.

East Dulwich has experienced countless changes since it was a hamlet in 1340 called Est Dilewissh. Unfortunately, the experiences of the fourteenth century residents were not recorded for posterity, but people who lived in SE22 in the twentieth century have provided an interesting insight into their lives including during the dark days of the Second World War.

It is important that present residents work with the East Dulwich Society to preserve all that is best in SE22 and to make East Dulwich a happy and healthy place for all who live and work in this interesting part of South London.

The first edition of this book was published in 2001. As it has been out of print for some time, and many people have moved into East Dulwich in the last few years, I am glad that Amberley Publishing wanted to publish a revised edition.

John D. Beasley
August 2010

A postcard, sent in 1915, shows a shelter at the west end of Goose Green.

A lamp-post and horse trough were surrounded by tramlines where the Goose Green roundabout is today.

Acknowledgements

On the day I returned the final proofs of *Peckham and Nunhead Remembered* to Tempus Publishing, I went to Chener Books in Lordship Lane (East Dulwich's only bookshop) and I mentioned the forthcoming book to Jason Goy who worked there. He suggested that I should compile *East Dulwich Remembered* so I must first thank Jason and also publisher David Buxton for immediately agreeing to publish the first edition of this book.

When I write books, I often ask my friend Gill Frost (former Treasurer of The Peckham Society and a trained teacher) to read the typescript and the proofs which she does with much skill. For her ideas and eagle eyes I am very grateful.

Without the assistance of many people this book could not have been produced. The pictures have come from various sources including people who have contributed their memories. Among the people whose help I appreciate, including some who have died since recording their memories or taking photographs, are: Maurice Alexander, Derek Austin, Valerie Austin, Jeffrey Avis, Stella Baker, May Barry, Irene Barton, H. T. Benton, Elsie Blenkey, Mary Boast, Reginald Bond, Polly Brierley-Jones, Christine and Derek Brock, Rose Brooks, Frederick Bullard, Frederick Butcher, Ian Cameron, Harry Chambers, Amy Chapman, Vera Conway, Scott Cordes, Joan Coxon, Nora Cullingford, Gary Cummins, Sheila Davidson, Kathleen Davis, Toby Eckersley, Celia Frazer, Peter Frost, Josephine Grant (Assistant Librarian, London's Transport Museum), Jon Gunson, Joseph Hack, Gladys Halley, Jeff Hancock (Librarian, Surrey CCC), Gillian Harding, Kathleen Harper, Sheila Hearsum, P. Hotchin, George Iggleden, Gillian Johnson-Flint, Umberto Jozwiak of Dulwich Jewellers, Stanley Kettel, Hilda Kors, Mary Lewis, Winifred MacKenzie, Don Mew, Leonard Moncrieff, Elsie Moody, Mishi Morath, Gwen Morris, J.G. Morris, Peter Morris, Margaret Orford, Kathleen Pickard, Brenda Pooley, Barbara and Norman Rawle, Jonathan Riddell (Assistant Curator, London's Transport Museum), Sonia Rodway, Janet Rose, Elsie Sheppard, Reg Simmonds, Dave Smith, Michael Smith, Ruth Smith, Grace Smith-Grogan, Frank Staples, Elsie Stukings, Nellie Thornton, Violet Tucker, Vera Vickers, Janet Watson, Susan Watson, Ron Woollacott and Joyce Woods. I acknowledge the *London Evening Standard* for pictures which appeared in *Hitler Passed This Way: 170 pictures from the London Evening News*.

I would welcome the opportunity to borrow any old photographs of East Dulwich which could then be copied and deposited in the excellent Southwark Local History Library. Without that library and its very helpful staff, *East Dulwich: An Illustrated Alphabetical Guide* could not have been written. That book provided information for some picture captions in this book.

Photographs and information on East Dulwich can be seen at Southwark Local History Library, 211 Borough High Street, SE1 1JA (020 7525 0232).

CHAPTER 1

Homes

An unknown lady stands at the entrance to
No. 22 Shawbury Road.

Chores were Hard Work

There had been so much change in home
heating. Our home had a kitchen range with
an oven at the side for cooking. The first job
each day was to remove cinders, blacklead
and polish the grate, then kindle a new fire
with wood and paper. There was a steel
plate to be cleaned with emery paper and
much 'elbow grease' and the hearth made
clean with water and white hearthstone.

How we dreaded coal deliveries! The
coalman dragged sack after sack of coal or
coke from the trolley and humped it through
the terrace house shedding dust and pieces of
coal as he went which he crunched over on
each journey – this meant a major clean-up.
He always seemed to arrive at meal times or
on rainy days. Looking back, there was the
joy then of sitting round a real fire enjoying
the beauty of real flames. The compensation
of today's heating is the immediate heat we

receive and the cleanliness of our homes now. Furnishings, walls and ceilings were quickly dirty from coal smoke.

Electric lighting too has made living so easy. We always had to have matches readily available as we groped through the house to the first gas burner. In bedrooms there was usually a small naked flame. In better rooms there was a burner bearing a mantle which was a fragile lace-like tube which fitted round a gas-jet to give incandescent light. I still wonder at the marvellous needlework produced under this poor lighting – especially when one remembers the long hours folk worked and how tired they must have been.

I remember washing days. We had a built-in copper in the corner of the scullery. The water was carried from the sink to the copper in a bowl and after the clothes had been removed from the copper the water was scooped out with a galvanised ladle fitted with a wooden handle. The fire had to be continually stoked. We burnt up newspaper, wrappings and garden rubbish, pushing it through a hole at floor level. It was very back breaking and the room would fill with steam as the clothes boiled. This was a job for us at lunchtime – there were no school dinners.

There were no easy care materials then. Clothes were hard to wash, dry and iron. They were dried, damped down and then ironed with a flat iron which was heated over a gas flame!

Violet Tucker in *Memories of the Good and Bad Old Days of Childhood*, contributed by some East Dulwich people (St John's church, 1976)

Baby Dead from Lead Poisoning

I was born on 4 April 1930 at No. 158 Upland Road. This house had been built in 1893 and was bought by my maternal grandfather. Their fourth child, a boy, was born there in the same year but he lived only nine days and cried all the time because he was born with lead colic (painters' colic), the house having been newly painted. My mother was born there at the end of the following year. Her father died in his forties from valvular disease of the heart when my mother was only eleven.

When the eldest son married, the house was divided into flats. The son and his wife lived downstairs; his mother and unmarried sister had the upstairs accommodation. When my parents married in 1929 they occupied the ground floor flat. This was where I was born the next year and my brother six and a half years later.

The front room was our drawing room, which had folding doors into the next room, but these were kept shut as this was our bedroom. This room had French doors, opening on to the passageway which led past the rest of the house to the garden.

I can remember sleeping in a cot – or crib as we called it – with dark polished wooden bars and a let down side. Later I had a proper bed. After my brother was born, these rooms were reversed, as the existing bedroom would scarcely hold a crib as well as a double and a single bed. That was the only time I can remember the folding doors being opened!

Next to this was the scullery, with a shallow yellow stone sink, a gas cooker and a mangle. We had only cold water, as the hot water system had failed and was never replaced, so every drop of water had to be heated on the gas stove, or in a kettle stood on a grid over the open fire.
Toast was made on the open fire too.

The room at the back, with a sash window looking out on to the garden, had been the kitchen but was now our dining room. We shared the bathroom and toilet upstairs,

Mrs Elizabeth Pooley (holding her dog) and her daughter-in-law Winifred Pooley, holding her son Donald, in the back garden of No. 77 Woodwarde Road, 1937.

Mrs Rose Chinneck and her granddaughter Brenda Pooley hold Donald Pooley in the back garden of No. 158 Upland Road, 1937.

although I remember using an enamel bath in the scullery.

Upstairs, grandma and auntie had the front room as a dining/sitting room. It was quite large as it extended over the hall as well as over our front room. It was from this room that I would watch the lamp-lighter, the muffin man with his bell and his tray on his head. Once I had the rare sight of a lorry with marionettes dancing on it. There was also the hurdy-gurdy man there, or in nearby streets.

Brenda Pooley, 2001

Owned very Little

I rarely pass St John's and St Clement's School in Archdale Road without some memory of those early days when I was a pupil there flooding back into my mind. If anyone had told me then that I would one day own a motor car, it would have seemed to me as remote as a fairy tale reminiscent of Cinderella becoming a princess or Dick Whittington the Lord Mayor of London.

We owned very little in those days. I lived with my mother and father in No. 6 Kent House, a small block of flats opposite the Epiphany Hall in Bassano Street. Our apartment, at the top of the block, had two rooms – a bedroom at the front and an 'everything else' room behind which had a garden made from the concrete roof of the flat underneath.

A brown stone sink was fitted into the corner by the back door and was surmounted by a single, brass tap from which we obtained cold water. Next to the blackened range in the chimney piece stood our 'new' cooker. My mother cleaned it diligently and frequently with a knife wrapped in an old cloth to get into the cracks, for it was not ours yet – it was still being paid for at the rate of *6d* a week.

Two ancient armchairs flanked the fireplace and were, no doubt, the result of some friendly transaction by my father. Their second or even third-hand shabbiness offered little comfort to those who walked across the threadbare mat between them.

Opposite the fireplace stood a scrubbed, wooden table surrounded by four odd chairs. On one of these hung my father's jacket when he was at home. It smelt of perspiration and putty. The pockets bulged with interesting things like string and chain, nuts, bolts, screws, a tobacco tin, cigarette papers, a little machine to roll fags in, a folded ruler and a plumb line. However tempting the contents, going through father's pockets was a sin we learned early not to commit!

At the far end of the room was mother's treadle sewing machine and next to that was a piece of furniture oddly out of keeping with the rest. It was a gramophone which had been given to my mother because she worked at His Master's Voice gramophone factory at the time of her marriage. The smell of oily newness was contained inside it for many years and could be savoured when the louvred doors in front of the speaker were opened to take part in all kinds of imaginative play. We had very few records. In fact, I remember only one. This had *Fred Fanackapan* on one side and *Ain't it Grand to be Bloominwell Dead* on the other!

Vera Conway, 1989

Brenda Pooley in the back garden of No. 158 Upland Road, 1931. Most of the toys were knitted by her grandma.

Brenda Pooley plays with her cousins Pat, Lorna and Kenneth and Roy Gaved in the back garden of No. 77 Woodwarde Road, in the 1930s.

Parallel Bars in Garden

I remember No. 48 The Gardens where my grandparents lived with the unmarried members of the family. The house was like a relic of the Edwardian period. As a little boy before the Second World War, it seemed very grand and I had to be on my best behaviour when visiting.

In the semi-basement there was a vast kitchen with sculleries and larders leading off it. The floor was covered with a heavy duty lino. An indulgent aunt allowed me to roller skate around the huge kitchen table! There was also a refrigerator which was quite rare in those days.

The Austin men were keep-fit fanatics so in the frame of the kitchen door there were iron rings to exercise on. In the garden was a set of parallel bars.

Derek Austin, 2001

Monday was Washday

Every Monday my Granny Wallace came from her home at Clapham Common to help with the washing, a major undertaking when I was a child. The two zinc baths were brought into the scullery. They and the sink were filled with water and the lid of the mangle was turned back to reveal the rollers ready for action. Into the sink went plenty of soap flakes, into the smaller zinc bath went the Dolly Blue Bag, and we were off! I loved being allowed to help on washing day. Once the clothes were washed, into the big bath of rinsing water they went. The whites had their extra dip of Dolly Blue and all finally were put through the mangle. I enjoyed the anticipation as I fed the items in, being careful that the rollers did not get a grip on my fingers. Then on turning the big handle – heavy breathing at this stage – the flattened laundry emerging at the rear, the water building up into the last few inches of

Vera Leuers (now Conway), on the right, sits on a zinc bath in the Bassano Street roof garden with her sister Jeanette and Colin, who lived in the two rooms next door to theirs, in around 1946.

clothes until – SPLOSH! What joy! Then the clothes were put out on the long washing line down the garden to blow dry and smell sweet, weather and our neighbour's bonfire permitting.

Sonia Rodway, 2001

Houses Lacked Amenities

I was very fortunate though I didn't realise it at the time; our house was all electric. We also had a bath, an indoor toilet, a bathroom and a coal cellar under the stairs and not under the house.

Some of my friends had a much harder life. They very often didn't even have hot running water. Some had an outdoor toilet and no bathroom. That was just the other side of Lordship Lane in Whateley Road and Silvester Road. Some houses had their coal poured down a hole, which had a black cast iron lid, in the front garden. Some children had no shoes.

Joyce Woods (*née* Mason), 2000

Moved into Prefab

Our last days in Bassano Street were heralded when my little sister became ill with appendicitis and the doctor had to be called. She was four years old then and I was almost ten. The doctor looked around and decided that our living conditions were becoming increasingly cramped and that we needed more room. He used his powers with the local council to get our names registered for a prefabricated bungalow. Prefabs were really built for those families who had lost their homes through the bombing but we were able to move into ours about a year later. We were, very considerately, placed as close as possible to all our familiar amenities and, specially important, not far away from gran and granddad. It was a longer walk from the shops and we were on top of a hill at No. 275 Lordship Lane, which became our new home. It was hard for mum to carry the daily shopping load up the hill, but years of humping water, shopping and sometimes extra fuel from Bicknell's Coal Yard in Whateley Road, whenever we needed it, had made her tough and there was always gran to help.

My sister was still too young to have become a 'street raker', as children who played in the street were called. Big changes were about to happen in the lives of all my friends as we prepared, by taking the eleven-plus examination, to leave St John's School for secondary education. My mother was thrilled with her new kitchen, which included a refrigerator (necessary because of the rather thin wall of the prefabs), a boiler, an electric cooker and more cupboard space than we were ever likely to need. We still needed coal and coalmen used to carry the hundredweights up the long path to our house, but we had a brand new purpose-built shed to keep it in, along with dad's gardening tools. For the first time in his life, he had a *real* garden ... a very big one too. The hard work that would be needed to change what was a veritable bombsite (on which the prefabs had been built) into a garden was nothing less than a wonderful challenge to him and he shifted piles of rubble almost single-handed.

Vera Conway, 2001

Food Delivered

The house I lived in had a black and white tiled path, and two big steps up to the front door. Every week Emma came to scrub and whiten them.

Mr Allen came on his bicycle with his basket of eggs. The United Dairies man brought a crate full of butter and cakes as well as milk (in quart and pint bottles.) A boy came from the grocer's to collect our order and returned with the food.

Brenda Pooley, 2001

Tin Bath Used

I was born in St Giles' Hospital, Camberwell, in 1927 while my parents were living in Chadwick Road following their marriage. By the time I was five, and had begun attending Grove Vale School, we had moved to No. 2 Chesterfield Grove.

We had the bottom half of the house and small backyard with an outside lavatory.

Work was done in the 1960s to prepare for building Dawson's Heights Estate.

I was bathed in a tin bath on the kitchen table. My parents went to Dulwich Baths as they had no bathroom. The cost of hiring huckaback towels was a penny a time.

My father was a bus conductor based at Nunhead Garage in Nunhead Lane, where my paternal grandparents lived at No. 73. My maternal grandparents lived at No. 270 Friern Road; my earliest memories are of visiting those homes. We walked up North Cross Road, where we always looked to see if there were any lost dogs tethered in the police station yard at the corner of Crystal Palace Road. We went across the diagonal path on Peckham Rye to the corner of Nunhead Lane. Wilson's fairground was nearby; it opened on Bank Holidays.

Christine Brock (*née* Edgar), 2001

At the age of twelve months I was walking all over the place. Before that I was crawling and climbing everywhere. One day my mother put me into a home-made playpen in the garden. After viewing me from the window several times, she carried on with her housework in our Fenwick Road house.

A short time later she was startled to learn that I was sitting on the kerb outside the King's Arms waiting to cross East Dulwich Road, presumably heading for the grass on Peckham Rye. A young woman neighbour had knocked on the door. 'Did you know your baby was out?' she kept shouting. My mother asked why she hadn't picked her up and brought her home.

My father had just arrived home. He rushed around the corner to the spot. I was still crawling up and down bewildered by the traffic. He picked me up saying, 'And where do you think you are going?'

I had managed to crawl out of the playpen, down the garden path, over the step of the back garden door and across the back passage. I then tumbled down a few stairs into the lower passage and through the downstairs front door which had been left ajar. I went up three stairs, through the front gate, across the road (luckily deserted), along the pavement opposite, around the corner and then paused at the kerbside watching the traffic go by! That was an amazing journey for so young a baby. Even though it was 1919 it was still a miracle that I was unhurt.

My mother certainly had an attack of the vapours that day but I can truthfully say that I can remember most of it.

Grace Smith-Grogan, 2001

Before moving to Dovercourt Road, my grandparents' home had been in nearby Beauval Road. My grandmother thought Dovercourt highly superior to Beauval so after their move would refuse to acknowledge that they had ever lived anywhere else. Indeed, she would scarcely utter the name Beauval, preferring instead genteel mouthing. To this day, we still refer to Beauval Road in mime.

My parents bought No. 94 Woodwarde Road; we moved there in April 1939 when I was four. This was a four bedroomed, halls-adjoining semi-detached house, with a deep porch and square bay front windows. I loved it.

In the summer the sideway was an ideal bowling alley for my brother as it was a narrow passage bounded on either side by the walls of our own and our neighbours' house. I refer, of course, to proper bowling as in cricket, not the ten-pin variety.

Our neighbours on the bowling-alley side were teachers and had a non-resident maid. They were good neighbours except on Mondays when they had a habit of lighting a bonfire which never seemed to consume anything but smoked miserably for most of the day and dirtied my mother's line of washing.

On the other side, in the house whose hall adjoined ours, the neighbours had a resident maid who always seemed to be overworked and careworn. Every afternoon the maid changed from her working clothes into her black dress with white cap and apron, ready to open the door to visitors.

Sonia Rodway, 1999

Comfortable Lifestyle

My friend and her family lived in a house in Devonshire Terrace, East Dulwich Road. Her father worked for the Moss empires so they enjoyed a comfortable lifestyle. They had a uniformed maid who waited at the table, a woman to do the housework and a gardener who came from Peckham Rye Park. My friend attended Clark's College. I was invited to one of her parties.

After tea her father sometimes took my friend and me to the New Cross Empire if there was a suitable programme on. This made a change from playing party games and we did so enjoy it.

There were quite a number of well-to-do people in East Dulwich and many private schools.

Grace Smith-Grogan, 2000

Lived Above Shops

We moved to No. 31 Lordship Lane in April 1941 after the house in Herne Hill – where I was born in 1936 – suffered bomb damage.

Next door to us was White & Sons photographic studios. George White and his wife Dorothy were friends of our family. Dorothy had worked with my mother in the post office.

Within two years we moved to No. 41 Lordship Lane because of dampness. As a baby I had suffered from bronchopneumonia and a weak chest. Each winter I had to wear a Thermagene Patch on my chest. It was heated in front of the coal fire and put on hot; the fumes from it helped my breathing.

Both Nos. 31 and 41 Lordship Lane were flats over shops. At No. 41 my mother Eva and father Frank slept on the ground floor in a room behind the shop. My brother Derek and I had a large room on the top floor next to the bathroom. When the bombing became really bad we all slept in the basement.

One night as we were preparing for bed I went down to the basement with an artificial cigarette which I had bought from a trick shop in Grove Vale. It had shiny red paper at the end which gave it a glow. Due to the cold weather, when I exhaled it looked as if I was smoking. Mum went spare.

Peter Morris, 2001

Plans to Demolish Homes

As the founder and secretary of LASH (London Association for Saving Homes) in 1973, I was trying to rally those who wanted to stand and fight against the bulldozer. The motto was 'Don't just do something, stand there'. A public meeting was called by Southwark Council in January 1975 at St Antony's Church Hall in Barforth Road to promote some bulldozing plans in the Nunhead area. I got wind of it but arrived a little late.

On the platform in the small hall were a number of luminaries including the then Chairman of Housing, Councillor Charlie Sawyer and the then Director of Housing, John O'Brien. The former expanded for several minutes about how marvellous life would be if the Nunhead demolition plans proceeded, how more dwellings would be created on the gardens of the demolished homes and then he ventured further:

'When we get round to East Dulwich,' he said, 'we will build 250 habitable rooms per acre' ... or whatever number was required by the Government directives then applying to slum clearance.

The words in quotes are precisely those he used and are seared in my memory. Fortunately for East Dulwich the tide turned in time.

Toby Eckersley, 2001

A young girl outside No. 12 Frogley Road, c. 1910.

Rodents Invaded

In the early 1970s our house at No. 178 Peckham Rye suffered from rodents, both large and small. Mice had always been a problem since we had moved there in 1969. We attempted to block up gaps beneath the skirting boards and between the floorboards, but the fact that we had multiple holes where pipes (water, gas and compressed air) and electric cables ran made our house a perfect haven for these furry creatures. Added to this was a constant food source, some dropped from our then infant children and also from our pet parrot's cage.

No packet, cardboard, cellophane or polythene proved a hindrance to these creatures with their well-designed incisor teeth. You could forget about placing food items on the top shelf of the larder, or even storing long-life food for camping holidays in the attic. The mice enjoyed the challenge of searching for items in the most out-of-the-way places.

Not content to make food security an impossibility, they also nested in the most obscure places, using all manner of materials. My old RAF 'housewife' (which those ancient enough will remember was a pouch with needles, cotton thread and wool used by generations of servicemen to darn their socks, and which I kept with our camping gear in the attic), fell victim to this home-making assault. Things had reached *Tom and Jerry*-like proportions and they showed themselves blatantly at every opportunity. We had mousetraps galore but the ultimate deterrent, poison, was difficult to administer because of the children.

In the garden we had made a sandpit where a flower bed had once been and we noticed that mysterious holes kept appearing, which we used to rake over. Persistently, they reappeared almost immediately. On further investigation, we found that they had developed into a maze of tunnels which interlinked like the subways beneath Piccadilly Circus.

At about this time I descended the stairs one morning only to have a sinking feeling on treading on the floor; I fell through the floorboards! We knew that the previous occupant had to have new joists and floorboards put in after he discovered that the original floor had been laid directly on to the earth but he had omitted this area. It had taken eighty years for this to manifest itself. What does one do with the earth beneath the joists? It had to be removed by hand to a depth of six inches below the joists and spread over the garden. Our front and back flower beds were all raised

Above left: Ron Woollacott drew this picture of No. 178 Peckham Rye as a gift for Peter Frost.

Above right: An unknown boy in the back garden of No. 158 Upland Road, *c.* 1900.

by about two inches with this red substance which resembled crushed bricks. Further extensions of the ratty Piccadilly Circus were discovered and the maturity of the tunnels suggested that they had been there for a generation (human one) or so. It was decided to fill the void beneath the floor with concrete after removing the rotten wood. Cables and wires were simply buried in this filling process as the builders had said that any new cables could go along the skirting board. Poison was placed in the rat holes before the concrete was poured. It seemed a good idea at the time.

The following morning I noticed that there had been an attempt at digging a hole in the hardening cement. I thought at first that it was a rat trying to come in, but it turned out to have been an imprisoned one trying to get out! A couple of days later a terrible

smell in the sitting room near the fireplace brought the builders back. They removed several floorboards and discovered, you've guessed it, more rat holes and a terrible stench. A rat had expired under the floor but was impossible to find and extricate. The builders decided to prepare a slurry of wet cement which was forced into the holes. The smell went!

Two other incidents can be recorded. One was when our telephone ceased to work. Examination of the cable indicated nibble marks. A more serious incident began when Gill, my wife, noticed a periodic flash going across the metal sink and draining boards. Then she received an electric shock from the sink unit. We contacted our electrician who was puzzled and decided to investigate further. Our newly-laid wood block floor had to be partially taken up in order to trace the wiring back to the fuse box. A dead rat was found with its teeth in the act of biting the electric cables. We were told that the electric shock would have been fatal if Gill had had her hands in water at the time.

The final part of the commentary on East Dulwich rodents was the marked increase in their activity during the dustmen's strike. A large dump of refuse existed where the hard standing used to be, opposite King's on the Rye*. There was also one on Goose Green. We heard that many houses were plagued by rats and in the house which was formerly the Southwark headquarters of the Red Cross, their entire stair carpet had been eaten away!

I hope that the more squeamish among the readers haven't been put off their food by my cautionary 'tail'.

Peter Frost, 2002

* now Rye Apartments

CHAPTER 2

Wartime

German POWs were housed in huts on Peckham Rye during the First World War. On nearby Goose Green soldiers performed their drills.

Watching Soldiers on Goose Green

When the war years came in 1914 we children used to look through high railings around Goose Green and watch the soldiers drilling, and there were horses and tents as well. Dulwich Baths was a soldiers' hospital and we would go and entertain the wounded. I remember playing draughts with a soldier who had lost an arm, and many others had lost their legs and had their heads bandaged. I used to blame God for everything, but I realise now it is not God's doing, but man's.

Elsie Stukings, 1976

Proud of War Wounds

In September 1939, I should have started to attend the Kindergarten of James Allen's Girls' School but Hitler decreed otherwise. We were on holiday on the Isle of Wight in August when my father, who was in the Territorial Army, was summarily recalled to his unit leaving us to 'enjoy' the remainder of our stay. Rumours abounded, and on one occasion we were en route to the beach when a distraught resident hastened down our garden path to tell us that Mr Chamberlain had just broadcast that we were now at war with Germany; no one was to go out without a gas mask and we had to pass on this message to anyone else we met. My mother dutifully carried out this request later, on the beach, to three fellows who responded with roars of laughter. So much at that early stage for Hitler! From the Isle of Wight we moved to Torquay for a short time, before returning home to East Dulwich.

JAGS Kindergarten was suspended for the duration of the war, so I did not become a pupil there until 1944, having sat the entrance examination in the school air raid shelter. I clearly remember the day of the exam. Mother and I set off from No. 94 Woodwarde Road and scurried from 'safe house' to 'safe house' of our neighbours and my grandparents. We paused at each one in case the siren went to give warning of an air raid.

This reminds me of somebody at that time who always referred to the 'Sireen'. Perhaps this was the upper class pronunciation but the same quality of bombs fell on them as on us! We were fortunate in that no bombs did fall on us personally, nor on our home, although dear No. 94 Woodwarde Road was slightly damaged on several occasions, with windows blown out and the violent descent of my bedroom ceiling, in my absence, I

hasten to add. I was, however, a casualty on one occasion, when a bomb did fall a little too close for comfort. My brother and I were at a party across the road at the house of my friend Elizabeth Banks. We had just finished tea and had moved from the front room to the back for party games, an ordeal for me equal to that of the teatime blancmange. Had we been greedy children, which we were not and impossible in any case, thanks to rationing – we might still have been indulging ourselves in the front room and safe. A bomb fell in Court Lane, which runs parallel with Woodwarde Road. The windows were blown in and broken glass rained down upon us, cutting my nose which bled profusely.

Confusion reigned. One of the boys, Howard King, suggested dropping a key down my back, a popular remedy then for nosebleeds; I can't think why. In any case my nose was bleeding from its cut exterior, so my brother nobly hastened up the road to fetch Dr Heard, who lived in one of the big houses near Dulwich Library. I can't remember, now, whether he was there, nor what was done to my nose, but I was subsequently quite proud of my scar, evidence of my war wound.

My poor parents were, at this time, celebrating one of my father's rare spells of leave, with our friends Frank and Kathleen Bailey, who kept the Fox Under the Hill public house on Denmark Hill. 'A bomb has fallen in Court Lane', reported an air raid warden in search of a drink. They couldn't get home fast enough to see if their offspring were safe and sound and were glad to find one unscathed and the other only slightly scathed though a little pale.

It was, for us children, only mildly alarming and rather exciting, even more so when boasting about the event at school and flaunting my war wound. It was not so funny for my parents. We were fortunate to suffer only minor household and personal damage. Many were bombed out and lost so much.

Air raids became an accepted part of our lives as the war got under way. In the early months, we sheltered in the cupboard under the stairs, where my mother kept on the shelf a special tin of sweets for air raids. I can remember a typical child's response of 'Oh goody – we can have a sweet?', whenever the siren went. Perhaps it might have been chocolate, had we been in the 'Sireen' class! This must have been before sweets, like almost everything else, were rationed and chocolate became only a memory.

Sonia Rodway, 1999

Wartime in Lordship Lane

When my mother, brother and I were returning home after having inoculations at Epiphany Hall in Bassano Street, we heard a V1 coming. As it crossed Lordship Lane its engine cut out. Mum pushed us into the doorway of an off-licence and we watched it go over a bank on the corner of Ashbourne Grove and then head towards North Dulwich. It dropped out of view and we heard the explosion.

The bombing of the Co-op in Lordship Lane was the worst as we were so close to it. My brother and I were in the basement of No. 39 playing with our neighbour's daughter. The whole place shook and many windows were broken.

In our dining room we had a quarter size billiard table. By the end of the war, the carpet was good at the edges and under the table, but worn through in between because we played so many games. Most weekends we had men from all three services and the Home Guard in our home; they enjoyed the billiards.

Very close to the end of the war, my cousin came one Sunday afternoon. His name was Jim Rowland and he was in the RAF. He flew Hawker Typhoons, a single-seater plane. Before the war he was at university studying to be a doctor. As he left our home, he told my Dad that he was due out on a mission on the following Wednesday but had a feeling that he would not return. In fact, he was shot down in Belgium. Local people rescued his body and hid it from the Germans. After the war, his parents went to Belgium to visit his grave. He had been buried with full military honours. Some of his personal effects were returned including a small pocket Bible with bullet marks on it.

Peter Morris, 2001

Slept in the Air Raid Shelter

Next to the Epiphany Hall, an air raid shelter had been built. We had a shelter behind the ground floor apartments, in our flats in Bassano Street but for some reason my parents preferred to use the public one. I remember the smell of the sacking which was used to line the rows of bunk beds along the lengths of the walls, the flickering lamps and torches, the enamel mugs of flask tea and the cheerfulness that barred anything like fear from entering my small head. I thought this was the norm; that life was always like this. The grown-ups said that one day the street lights would be lit again, that we would not have to black out or put out that light and we would be able to sleep in our own beds every night and not have to go to the shelter. One day daddies would come home and we could have bananas and food would be plentiful again. I remained unconvinced by any of these promises; this was the only life I knew.

A flying bomb destroyed the Royal Arsenal Co-operative Society's store at Nos. 111-115 Lordship Lane, as well as neighbouring shops, on 5 August 1944. There were many people in the shops and a queue of passengers waiting at the tram stop outside. Twenty-three people were killed and forty-two seriously injured.

Most of my friends had Anderson shelters in their gardens. Gran and granddad had a public brick shelter right outside their front door, where it was parked like a car at the roadside. They rarely used it as they preferred to 'take a chance' and stay indoors. Fortunately, they passed unharmed through the war years. During the worst of the raids I had to share a top bunk with an elderly woman from Blackwater Street. Her pillow was at one end of the bunk and mine at the other. She complained, saying that she could not sleep properly because I kicked her in the night!

The 'Chinese Lanterns' that grew by the door to the shelter afforded much fascination for me. They grew wild and I suppose that nobody else noticed them, but even now the plant reminds me of our life in the air raid shelter.

Vera Conway, 2001

Collected Gas Masks

During Christmas 1937, and the early weeks of January 1938, the weather was bitterly cold and frosty, with heavy snowfalls imparting a magical look to all the trees and shrubs in Peckham Rye Park. Children and dogs were happily playing in the snow and everything seemed so peaceful and secure that fears of war faded into the background.

Sadly, this sense of false security was soon to end, when Germany marched into and annexed the independent state of Austria. Alarm bells were metaphorically ringing. I went up to London one Saturday to find soldiers digging deep trenches in Hyde Park and piles of sandbags being placed strategically outside all the hotel entrances. There was talk of war on every side and when all citizens were told to report to designated places to collect their gas masks, it seemed inevitable.

My mother and I went together to Dulwich Baths to obtain our masks, and it was a nightmare scenario! Little children were crying and screaming as the masks were forced over their faces to ensure they were a good fit. We stood waiting in the slow moving and anxious queue for a very long time. The masks were clumsy to handle and the smell of rubber was overpowering. In no time at all the eyepiece was rendered almost useless by condensation from the breath of the wearer and the perspiration quickly engendered by the close fit of the mask did not help matters. Also, in my own case, there was an unpleasant sense of claustrophobia. However, we clung to them with gratitude at the thought that they might be the only means of saving our lives in the event of a gas attack. I wondered what would happen to our animals in such an event.

Joan Coxon, 2001

Nights Spent in the Shelter

The majority of children were evacuated to the country during the war but apart from a short time staying with my aunt in Newcastle at the end of the war, I stayed at home as did several other children in the road. I can remember the many nights spent in the Anderson shelter at the bottom of the garden. It had two tiers of three bunks and steps down from the small opening. There was a thick layer of earth over the top to help give extra protection but dad used to grow vegetables there as he had to grow as much food as possible and not much space was wasted. I remember it was always a bit of a skirmish getting into the shelter as there was always someone behind saying 'Hurry up there's a plane coming!' and there was sometimes water in the bottom so we had to get straight on to a bunk without getting our feet wet. All

In 1945 a street party was held in Bassano Street to celebrate the ending of the Second World War.

this before the candle was lit! Sometimes the raids would start before we could get to the shelter so the youngest of us would spend the night under the kitchen table. We had great faith in that table which had huge turned legs and a thick scrubbed deal top. If we were having a meal and we heard a bomb coming down everyone would shout 'duck!' and we would all drop to the floor with our heads under the table. We used to laugh to think how we must have looked with all our bottoms sticking out round the table. Mum would not go to the shelter without her bag which contained all the important things like the rent book, ration books, insurance books and housekeeping money and I used to grab the cat and he came too. I can remember when a landmine dropped behind the houses opposite us; it did not explode. It took ages for the army to defuse it and dig it out as we understood there was an underground stream there. All the people on that side of the road were told to share the shelters of the neighbours opposite, so for many nights in our shelter there were two families plus their dog and our cat. Nearly everyone sat up all night but come the morning everyone got on with the normal day, as did everyone else through the war.

Gill Harding, 2001

Pigs Kept

When I look back at my East Dulwich days, it seems that I spent many more years there than I actually did, such has been the effect upon me throughout my life. Of the thirteen years spent at No. 94 Woodwarde Road, six were overshadowed by war. At the beginning of hostilities, an Anderson air raid shelter was established in one of Alleyn's School's playing fields which adjoined some of the rear gardens of Woodwarde Road. Our garden just missed direct contact with this field, but Mr and Mrs James kindly removed some palings from the fences, thus allowing us to nip smartly along to the shelter when the warning went. Further down the road lived dear Mr Collar, who was so concerned at the plight of my mother with her two temporarily fatherless children that, at the first note of the siren, he would hasten to escort us all to safety. I remember him clearly and recall that he always seemed to be properly attired in suit, collar and tie, no matter what the time of the air raid. The siren was a truly dreadful sound and evoked the feeling so passionately expressed many years later by Private Fraser in Dad's Army that we were 'doomed – DOOMED!'

The all-clear was quite a different sound – one high bright cheerful note of assurance that all, for the time being, was well. Eventually, we acquired our own Morrison Shelter, a solid steel rectangular affair which occupied almost the whole of the kitchen. It wasn't very high, so we crawled on all fours and wriggled into the bedding as best we could. My mother and I lay one way and my brother the other, he and I complaining bitterly of being kicked or suffering hideous feet in our faces. These horrors were far worse than any threat from Hitler. I can't imagine how my poor mother managed to make the bed but manage she did. Her own experience of a night of particular terror was caused, not by falling bombs or gunfire, but by a mouse. She woke to the sound of gnawing at the door to the scullery. Bravely crawling from the security of the shelter, she seized the nearest item and stuffed it into the gap under the door. Come the morning, she was not a little dismayed to find her vest considerably more lacy than when she took it off. We never found the mouse – perhaps it expired with indigestion. Apart from feet, mice, the siren, falling bombs, overhead aircraft and Ack-Ack gunfire, our rest was further disturbed by the sound of shrapnel raining down, often noisily hitting the dustbin. The largest pieces of shrapnel became close rivals to the largest conkers, both gleefully collected by us children. Conkers were an important part of our war effort, on the home front that is, as they formed part of the staple diet of pigs, some of whom were reared singly by individual households then, and were, when the fateful day came, enjoyed as a welcome supplement to the rations. My nose, as I write, is wrinkling in distasteful memory of the pig bins which were placed at intervals along many roads (though not, as I recall, in Dovercourt, oh my dear life no!). These were for the collection of household waste, such as vegetable peelings and were often overflowing.

To return to the conkers, I remember my mother, brother and me collecting vast numbers of these in Dulwich Village and College Road, some for the pigs and some for my brother Peter to use in the time honoured fashion. To this end, on one occasion some were baked in the oven to render them even harder than nature intended. Unfortunately, they exploded before they could be put to the test. On one of my later pilgrimages to Dulwich I couldn't resist bringing home a beautiful specimen from the lovely trees in the Village, a 'sixer' at least. I wonder whether conkers were ever fed to the two splendid pigs who resided in a pen in one of JAGS playing fields. This must have been in around 1944; often in my lunch break I used to pop up and visit them, leaning over the wall of their sty to scratch their backs. I do hope they never supplemented our school dinners, although certainly they began for me a lifelong love of pigs. They are such jolly creatures, aren't they?

There was little that, at some point, was not rationed during those years. Food, of course, was rationed, even bread, sweets and clothes. There was sometimes one egg per child per week, in addition to the dried egg powder, which was quite palatable when scrambled – unlike dried milk which I loathed. Very little could be obtained without the appropriate number of points in our ration books – I still have mine – and clothes required a certain number of clothing coupons, or 'kewp'ns' as one shopkeeper referred to them, while another, much more refined, always gave them a French pronunciation. I doubt that the merchandise varied whether kewp'ns or cou-pons were proffered.

Sonia Rodway, 2001

Bomb Killed Neighbours

The Blitz started on 7 September 1940 and our block of flats, Goldwell House, was bombed eight days later. At No. 15 lived the Moakes family who did not like the shelters so when the bomb hit our flats they were killed.

We moved just across the road to No. 1 Constance Road (now St Francis Road). I will always remember 12 July 1944. I was kicking a ball around in my road and then heard the drone of a V1 flying bomb. Its engine cut out and I saw it flying over the council flats, down Quorn Road and over my head. I was petrified. I heard it hit St Francis Hospital and there was a very big bang. Most of the windows in our road were being smashed. The blast picked me up and threw me into the bottom of Dog Kennel Hill. My nose was bleeding, ears ringing and my breathing was bad. I crawled to the kerb and, with my coat sleeve, I cuffed the blood from my nose. I walked to the Cherry Tree pub and called out to my mum and dad. Dad said, 'Harry boy, you caught the bomb blast'.

A street party was held in Chesterfield Grove as part of the VJ Day celebrations in 1945.

During the war I had two paper rounds – St Francis Hospital in the morning and the big houses in Dulwich village in the evening. I also made money from chopping up bomb damaged doors and picking up apples from the big houses and making toffee apples which I sold to kids on a little stall I set up.

H. T. Benton, 2001

Tank for Fire Fighters

At the west end of Goose Green inside the railings a very large tank was installed containing water for use in emergency by firefighters during the Second World War. It was quite a while before it was dismantled.

Grace Smith-Grogan, 2001

Music Raised Spirits

The piano was the focal point of many of our wartime entertainments. On Sunday evenings my mother would play and the three of us children still at home would sing.

My father, apart from periods of leave, was absent for all six years of the war, helped I feel sure by my nightly pleas to the Almighty to 'Please bless Daddy and help him knock Hitler scatty'.

The musical evenings raised our spirits considerably and we hugely enjoyed them. I still have the *Daily Express Song Book* from which my mother played.

Sonia Rodway, 1999

Collected Shrapnel

Now aged seventy-two, I lived in No. 192A Lordship Lane from the age of one until we moved to No. 421 Lordship Lane in 1939.

When the Crystal Palace was on fire, my mother woke me up and I saw the autogiro circling the inferno.

In around 1938 I witnessed meetings of the blackshirts (fascists) and the infamous Joyce family outside the Queen's Pantry which was opposite Dulwich Library. The Joyce family lived in Allison Grove, SE21.

As an evacuee I walked from Grove Vale School to East Dulwich station with a gas mask and label with my name on it en route to Mickleham near Dorking – only to return to Lordship Lane in December 1939 in time for the air raids.

From Dawson's Hill I saw the bombing of the London Docks at the start of the Blitz. I saw dogfights and bombers going over. Later in the war I witnessed our bombers going to Germany signalling their V for victory sign.

I heard and watched V1s (doodlebugs) close at hand. One night Etherow Street was demolished by a landmine which also blew the window of our house out and destroyed the roof. On the site of the carnage, prefabs were erected which were later replaced by council housing.

There was little schooling in those days. As boys our main hobby was collecting shrapnel, nose cones from shells etc., usually from Dulwich Park after almost nightly raids.

Don Mew, 2000

Treats Enjoyed During War

In reality, school was becoming more fun than it had been for me at that age, even in Mrs Mortleman's class! We looked forward to playtime in what seemed to us to be that enormous playground! We played 2 balls against the walls and became quite adept at juggling. We were often to be found upside down, showing our navy blue, fleecy lined drawers with all important elastic at the waist and legs, doing handstands or cartwheels. There were games of 'peep behind the curtain' and 'witches' or 'watering cans' (the game in which spitting was apparently allowed!) into which we entered with all enthusiasm, except perhaps in the depth of winter when the toilets froze solid and we tried to keep warm in our knitted bonnets, thick lisle stockings and Peter Pan bodices! No one said 'ugh' to a mugful of milk heated before the open coal fire in wintertime. We paid our ½d, peeled off the skin and drank it thankfully!

The problem of where to find little treats for us, especially at Christmas time, never defeated the staff at St John's School. Sweets were rationed as well as being in short supply, but once we were given ice cream cones filled with marshmallow and dipped in coconut. On another occasion we had to take saucers and spoons to school with us for our share of the jelly sent to the school from America. It was made up in the school kitchen and testing it was a new experience for us, as table jellies were not on sale in England during the war years. From the same source came a supply of drinking chocolate powder; we were given a measure each in a screw of paper, but most of it was eaten before it ever got to being added to a cup of milk! Thinking of food reminded me of the baker's shop opposite the school. It was on the corner of Fellbrigg Road, and the glorious smell of baking cakes and bread was the first impression of the outside world that we received upon leaving the school gates! Bread and cakes were rationed too, and the appropriate coupons had to be submitted with the price, but somehow the fairy cakes were exempt! They were indeed small and shaped like shells. They were delicious and could be eaten by the starving ones in two mouthfuls! They cost ½d each!

Vera Conway, 1989

Bricks Blown on to Bed

I was born on 7 June 1917 at No. 3 Waveney Avenue but I spent most of my youth in Barforth Road. I attended Friern School from 1922 until 1928 when, having won a Junior County Scholarship, I went on to Haberdashers' Aske's Hatcham Boys' School. At Friern School there was a special class in the charge of Mr Cowan which prepared selected pupils for Junior County examination.

In the early 1930s we moved to No. 7 Drakefell Road, New Cross. We were a family of five as I had twin brothers. We were bombed out of Drakefell Road early in the war. My parents and I then moved to a top floor flat over what is now Burnet, Ware and Graves estate agent's offices on the corner of Peckham Rye and East Dulwich Road. We were also bombed out of there. The blast blew bricks on to my bed in a room facing the King's Arms, but fortunately I wasn't in it at the time.

We then secured a house at No. 5 Dovedale Road which had been evacuated by two lady schoolteachers.

Maurice Alexander, 2000

Babies Given to Mothers

I was born in Dulwich Hospital in 1944. My mother told me that when an air raid siren sounded, all the babies were given to their mothers. Normally, the babies were kept in a nursery away from their mothers.

As a delayed action bomb had recently landed in our garden and blown up the back of our house, my parents had temporarily rented a flat on Dog Kennel Hill overlooking King's College sports ground (where St Francis Park, Edgar Kail Way and Sainsbury's car park are today).

Gillian Johnson-Flint, 2000

Wartime Baby, 1944

Long dark days of wartime
Years of fiery storm
Battles over, battles defeated
Still the warheads come
Oh tired England wracked with pain
and abject misery
Yet mirth lifts its weary head
from this suffering Earth.

Out of the Holocaust
appear bright summer rays
Flowers unfold their tight curled buds
to greet the living days
Guns still boom and missiles drop
upon this summer scene
A terrifying stillness
dark smoke where life has been.

Into our strife torn world
emerged a baby boy
The sadness of the noisy air
his grave young eyes observe
Our little son so innocent
beneath his silky curls.
Oh stop the wailing siren
away with V2's hum
Our baby is trying to sleep
beneath the soothing sun.

Grace Smith-Grogan, 2000

Pupil Killed

One day we all had to squash up so that the rest of the St John's Junior School could come into our classroom to receive some special news of a sad and serious nature. We heard from the headmistress that one of our fellow pupils had been killed when his friend set light to an old mattress in the entrance to a dug-out shelter on the bomb site where the Co-op used to be, so trapping him inside. We

A victory party was held in Nutfield Road after the Second World War.

were warned not to speak about the incident to the young one who had made so serious a mistake, so as not to cause him further pain. The headmistress dwelt for some time on the perils of playing with matches and fire. We took it all very seriously. Those were heavy days. The anxieties of our parents hung over us and although we didn't understand war and all that it entailed we were serious children in between the fun.

Vera Conway, 1989

What a Match!

On Saturday mornings we all went to the pictures where I and lots of other children were Ovaltineys. My nan treated me to the pictures if I helped her to do some chores.

Oh yes, those were the days! Even the war years were fun for us as it was like an adventure. Railings were taken down and shelters were built – Anderson in back gardens and Morrison indoors with public ones in the streets. We had one at the bottom of our garden and a public one at the end of our street, Bassano Street.

I remember when a parachute mine was dropped, which demolished Lytcott Grove and Playfield Crescent. My granddad struck a match to light his pipe at the same time as the blast, and said 'Crikey, that was a strong match!'

Joyce Woods (née Mason), 2000

Pram Destroyed

In 1944, while I was awaiting the birth of my baby son, I was sent to Yorkshire from Dulwich Hospital as V1 flying bombs were raining down non-stop day and night over London.

On leaving Yorkshire, I journeyed with my two week old baby to stay with some old family friends in Oldham, Lancashire, for a short time. My lovely Marmot pram with nappies, mattress, pillow and sun canopy was being sent to Oldham by railway. It never reached there as the carrier van was blown up in Lordship Lane and I believe the driver was killed.

My pram was a mangled wreck. Only the nappies survived but they were as black as soot and full of tiny burn holes. As I had used up my quota of clothing coupons I could not obtain any more.

Grace Smith-Grogan, 2000

Woken By Gunfire

We were woken up by the sounds of thunder – only it wasn't thunder, it was gunfire. My younger sister and I were born just before the First World War and our mother used to put us to bed upstairs until we woke up and cried out, when she brought us down and laid us on a sofa, where we obviously felt safe and went off to sleep again. If the noise of gunfire got too loud we would all crowd under the kitchen table. I remember once my mother had opened a tin of bully beef – a treat – when a raid started and we ate it under the table. Another memory is of mother giving us each a rock cake with strict instructions to stay in bed while she went off to queue for food – rationing was not introduced till nearly the end of the war. On Armistice Day my father took us to Peckham Rye where bonfires were lit – there were crowds and I was frightened by a boy rushing about with a horrible mask on.

In 1918, my mother fell victim to the post-war flu. As she recovered she fancied a boiled egg. My twelve-year-old sister boiled the egg but boiled it hard. It was the only egg in the house! Food was still short and mother was dexterous at dividing a boiled egg between two of us – she would hit it smartly in the middle and pop the halves into two eggcups without spilling a drop of yolk.

Hilda Kors, 1976

Firemen Killed

Before I was called up in November 1940, I was in a first-aid post in the church hall on the corner of Townley Road and Lordship Lane. On our training sessions we had to manhandle the metal stretchers in and out of the bunkers. Afterwards they were used as railings around Council flats; some can still be seen in Camberwell Church Street.

The most frightening call-out was to the school in Grove Lane, near Denmark Hill station. The school had been converted into an auxiliary fire station. The firemen had taken shelter in bunkers in the playground but it received a direct hit and all twenty were killed. As they were dug out, we tried to revive them. However, the two firemen who had remained in the school were the only survivors.

Joseph Hack, 2001

Bomb Fell at Dulwich Hospital

In 1944, when I was heavily pregnant with my first and only child, I visited the clinic at Dulwich Hospital for my monthly check-up. Suddenly a bomb fell in the hospital grounds at the back. Smoke and dust poured in. About a dozen of us rushed for the door and headed for the front gates, followed by a nursing sister who yelled, 'Where on earth do you think you are going?' The reason for the question was that we were only wearing flimsy white gowns open at the back with no fastenings and there was a soft breeze blowing! No damage to the hospital was reported.

Grace Smith-Grogan, 2000

Watched Films at the Odeon

Next to the Grove Vale School there was a cinema called the Pavilion. My mother attended the opening. We children were allowed to go if the film was suitable. The Pavilion was demolished in 1935 and the Odeon was built on the site. This was beautifully furnished with lovely stage curtains patterned with large butterflies.

My fiancé and I would sit on the back row with all the other courting couples. This was wartime. Suddenly a message would flash on to the screen, 'An air raid is now in progress ... if you wish to leave please go quietly'. Immediately there would be a great banging of the folding seats as people rushed from the building. We nearly always stayed to the end however.

One night while watching a war film it was difficult to tell whether the guns and bomb explosions were coming from the screen or outside. When I finally arrived home I endured a ticking off from my father who thought I should have hurried home because if we were to be bombed we should all go together.

Grace Smith-Grogan, 2000

CHAPTER 3

Education

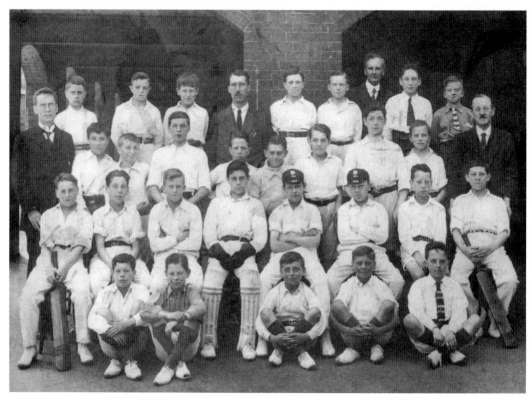

The Grove Vale School cricket team, 1923. Fifteen-year-old George Smith-Grogan is in the centre wearing the wicket-keeper's pads.

Attended Grove Vale School

I was a pupil at Grove Vale School from around 1916-1919. I remember the iron cups fixed to the wall with chains and the cold water taps. We used to swing the cups violently against the wall to make as much noise as possible.

Our family moved to Peckham when my father returned from France in 1919 after he had served in the First World War. My brother Sidney, who was two years older than myself, used to come home from Grove Vale School (before I had started there) and sang 'Sweet and low, sweet and low, winds of the Western Sea' to me which made me feel I

Boys from Grove Vale School with headmaster Mr Anderson and sports master Mr Haley (wearing a watch chain), *c.* 1938. In the background are the Odeon Cinema and Tintagel Crescent.

wanted to go to his school too.

Our little great-granddaughter used to attend the nursery class in what is now Goose Green School.

Margaret Orford (formerly Minnie Pellett) – St Leonards, East Sussex, 2000

First Day at School

My mother expected trouble over my having to go to school. From the time before my sister was born I had enjoyed considerable freedom, often going out by myself or playing in the streets. It was plain that I would not take easily to the idea of being cooped up in a classroom. Besides, my mother's own schooldays from 1908 onwards had not left her with happy memories, so perhaps her threat 'If you don't behave yourself, you'll go to school', prepared me somewhat negatively for the impending experience. I hated the

very idea of going to school and my mind was quite made up – I would not go.

The day for starting school inevitably arrived. The novelty of the unfamiliar ritual of morning preparations and new tensions overwhelmed all previous ideas and thoughts.

We stopped at Mrs Wilcox's greengrocer's to buy vegetables on the way – that was a comforting part of our normal routine. But then we continued up North Cross Road to St John's School. My mother took me into the classroom. This was situated in the bungalow building and we entered by the door next to the water taps. As we went up the steps we passed a tiny cloakroom off to the right where there were washbasins and pegs for the children's coats. The room we entered seemed enormous to me then. It was already full of children sitting on small wooden chairs, two at each table all facing the front. I was also shown to a similar chair and also given a book to read. My mother left after a few words with the teachers. If I shed any tears that day I do not remember them. The storms began later.

Vera Conway, 1989

Life at JAGS

When I did eventually start at James Allen's Kindergarten in September 1944, there were of course still some months of war to be waged. Therefore, at the beginning of each term, pupils were required to bring a supply of 'iron rations', in case they were detained at school by an air raid. It was considered a great joy, at the end of term, in addition to being released for the holidays, to consume these on the way home. I can't recall the contents of my box, apart from dry biscuits and an Oxo cube. Ghastly! Eating in public in school uniform was strictly forbidden, so the nibbling and munching had to be done with the furtiveness which comes naturally to most children!

School rules were strict. Gloves had to worn with long coats. Girls must not walk more than three abreast. Girls may not wait at the bus stop used by the Alleyn's boys' school. And so on.

I have very mixed memories of my years at James Allen's Girls' School. There are feelings of great pride and gratitude that I was able to attend such a school, but those feelings are stronger reflectively than they were at the time. My schooldays were clouded, to some degree, by fear of certain teachers. For example, in Domestic Science, our teacher was liable to lose her temper and hurl the cooking equipment in all directions. I think now that she suffered a disability and doubtless the ineptitude of some of her pupils exasperated her beyond endurance. 'I'm sorry', I quavered, during an early lesson, 'I've made my pastry too wet'. Surprisingly, neither my pastry nor I were thrown across the room. Some years later, in that same room, I concealed in the store cupboard the excess batter I had made for my ambitious School Certificate dessert of Berlin Pancakes.

Fifth formers at James Allen's Girls' School, 1949.

Alleyn's School opened on the present site in 1887.

In spite of that, and the voluminous cotton knickers we were required to create in needlework class, I passed.

The music teacher also struck terror into my heart for my first few terms. I was not (and am not!) musically able, and used to sit shaking with apprehension that I would be the one chosen to 'come and transpose the key of G'. I had no idea what 'transpose' meant, never mind how to do it. Had I been taught to transpose? I remember only the frightening figure of my teacher expecting me to know. She was succeeded, before too long, by a much kinder soul. My lack of talent did not prevent my enjoyment of music, and indeed I was admitted to the choir, quite how I know not, though I must allow myself a little credit in that I had a clear (small) voice and could sing in tune. I loved singing and have happy memories of choir practice in the music room with its raked floor, young voices soaring under the direction of our gentle teacher. One Founder's Day, in the College Chapel in Dulwich Village, we sang 'Jesu, Joy of Man's Desiring.' I shall never forget it. I have only to hear the introduction to that exquisite anthem to feel again the heart-moving anticipation I first knew so many years ago.

Who else do I remember? My first sports mistress! How scornful she was of us duffers who could not whizz forehands and backhands across the tennis net as to the manner born, nor shin up the ropes to the sickeningly high ceiling of the gymnasium. At the end of each term we were granted the treat – a dubious one, in my case – of playing in the gym a game called 'Pirates.' This entailed being pursued and having to evade capture by leaping, scrambling or swinging about on the equipment without touching the floor. If you did, you were out and never did I experience such relief as when my foot was seen to touch down. I did try, truly; I didn't cheat! And I wasn't entirely without sporting inclination. I was quite a nippy little right winger and did play hockey for my House, Desenfans, which was named after Noel Desenfans, an art collector and benefactor of the Dulwich Gallery.

There were subjects I did enjoy, mainly English and French. I remember in my oral examination for School Certificate endeavouring to inform my examiner that 'mon frère' was doing his National Service, quite how I translated that I shudder to think; I suppose 'Service Nationale' with a passable accent and an air of bravado must have got me through.

Another of our teachers, the art mistress, was also rather fierce but, strangely, I never had any fear of her even though I was entirely without artistic talent. She would often sketch one of us when we were working on our own. She sat at the high teacher's desk on the dais, frowning in concentration, tongue firmly in cheek. And now I can put it off no longer, I must face up to the headmistress! How formidable she seemed to me, with her austere authority and her grey hair severely confined into a bun. She taught mathematics and woe betide any girl unable to multiply 17½ x 37½ in an instant in her head! She had a habit, if an answer was not immediately forthcoming, of turning to the next pupil and in a tone of weary despair saying, 'Tell her, Daphne' (or Jean, or some other bright spark). This was hardly encouraging to anyone not entirely confident in areas mathematical. I was adequate and might have done better with encouragement rather than withering sarcasm. However, there came the happy day when, from the top division (why I was there in the first place I shall never know) I whizzed to the bottom, not even stopping at the middle! Such a relief! In the bottom division there was such a dear, wise and encouraging teacher who gave such kindly instruction. 'Well done' or 'Not quite right, but you're on the right lines'. My headmistress had still to be faced on other occasions, of course. I had only to hear her during morning prayers utter the dreaded phrase, 'A girl was seen' to flush crimson with guilt, although I never was the girl who had been seen! It was also a nerve-racking experience to be summoned to the head's study, quaking, awaiting the summons within, even if only for a minor misdemeanour, such as hair long enough to touch one's collar and not tied back! Anyone guilty of this offence had to spend the rest of the day with their hair tied back with string. Nevertheless, JAGS gave me a lot to enjoy and value, and laid the foundations of my love of words and music.

It is good to be an old JAGS girl and to have been part of the Edward Alleyn Foundation, as were my brother, Peter, our father and his brother who all went to Alleyn's School. My brother, while working in the school archives, came across a letter from my grandfather, written in the 1920s to the then headmaster of Alleyn's, requesting a school place for my Uncle Geoffrey.

I still have my school reports, both from Glenshee, mostly very good and from James Allen's – some of which the less said the better. No mention was made in any report of the occasion on which, at the start of a hockey match, I 'bullied off' too enthusiastically and whacked the nose of my opponent who was led weeping from the field!

How fortunate were we then, and pupils of today, to enjoy those vast areas of playing fields, as well as areas for botany studies

– the heath, the pond and the vegetable gardens. There was always school-grown produce for sale on Friday afternoons. I especially remember the splendid carrots, tops and all and the smell of the soil still clinging to them. I wasn't as enthusiastic when my name was down for gardening during the lunch break, at which we all had to take a turn. As with the dreaded tennis, I used to pray for rain.

No such prayers on idyllic summer days, when fifth formers preparing for matriculation exams were allowed to study out of doors and sat beside the pond declaiming their Shakespeare to the accompanying sound effects of the croaking frogs.

Another of my happy memories is the year I took part in the school play. In my day, this was performed in the hall and only certain classes were eligible, so there were limited opportunities to take part. I was then in the third form and my role was in an original nativity play, written by one of the teachers. I have only three memories of it. One is of proclaiming in ringing tones 'Lord God of Israel, Isaac and Abraham ...!' The rest of my lines have faded into oblivion. Another memory is of sitting on the draining board in the domestic science room washing the brown make-up off my legs. The third memory and the most remarkable is of my headmistress observing to my parents: 'Your child did well'.

The present-day purpose-built Prissian Theatre, which is the venue for more ambitious and more frequent productions, is much to be envied by us Old Girls, as is the wonderful library with its wide selection of books and quiet bays with tables for private study. What a far cry from the modest room which housed the school library in my day, where on Friday afternoons I blissfully browsed before making my choice from what was then a wealth of books available to us lucky children.

I now confess that the library was the scene of a shameful debacle for me, and two or three of my friends, when aged about fourteen. JAGS girls were not permitted to leave the school premises during the lunch break but the boys from Alleyn's were, and some would find it necessary to pass along East Dulwich Grove, this being clearly observed from the ideally situated window of our library. On this particular occasion we espied some of our heroes and were gaily waving, even perhaps calling a greeting, all naturally in a most ladylike manner, when we heard the door open. There stood our headmistress. Not a word was spoken. My blood, and doubtless that of my friends, ran cold. She stood aside as we slunk out. In due course, each of us was summoned to her presence to be lectured on the good name of the school and our own personal shame. Suitably chastened, we reflected what idiots we were to forget that the headmistress' study was immediately beneath the library!

I was involved, inadvertently I assure you, in another sorry incident, concerning a crab apple. There was, in the JAGS grounds, a beautiful tree which bore a splendid crop of enticing fruit. On the occasion I recall, I was passing this tree and, without thinking, I picked one rosy crab apple and ate it. 'Sonia Rodway! What do you think you are doing?' It was the voice of the gardening mistress, quivering with shock. I was given an instant detention, the ultimate disgrace.

The JAGS system of punishment and discipline, depending on whether it was being suffered or applied, was a 'Report' of minor misdemeanours, three of which automatically led to a detention. To receive the latter straight off was mortifying, even more so when I had to confess to my form mistress as was required. I dare say, these days, parents might take it amiss that their child had been reprimanded, but in my day,

Peter Hughes with his class at St John's School in the early 1950s.

when explaining to parents that you were to be kept in after school you got another ticking off.

Sonia Rodway, 1999

Wanted a Bible

My first classroom in St John's Junior School was situated through the second door at the top of the iron staircase, which, incidentally, I see has now been removed and I wonder if any accidents happened on it before it was actually taken away. I feared to go up it at first and found it nerve-racking to look down through the square holes in the treads, but we all grew used to the experience and I expect it helped us to develop heads for heights! Our behaviour on the iron staircase was, of course, exemplary

as we walked up and down it in silence. The first room at the top was occupied by Miss Good and her class. Miss Good was an elderly lady of whom it was said that she had spent almost her whole lifetime at St John's School in one capacity or another. The only years she had been away were the two spent at training college. When I knew her, she was close to retirement and I remember a kindly, bent lady wearing dark clothes with an oval face framed by two grey plaits which were looped and pinned around her ears. Occasionally, we went into her room for handwork lessons which usually meant making little models of chairs or tables from squares of coloured sticky paper, with the whole class folding simultaneously, or small woolly balls made by wrapping lengths of wool over the waxed cardboard lids from inside the tops of milk bottles. These lids had holes in the centre where the thumb had to press to get the lid out. (They were discontinued because they were no protection against the dust and dirt from the rim of the milk bottle.)

My own teacher at that time was Miss Strutt whom I remember as a friendly, communicative lady whose classroom practice was a little more relaxed than that of other teachers without any loss of discipline. Putting that another way – I enjoyed being in her class and was not afraid of her; she dealt with us all as individuals and we felt that her personal interest in each one of us was genuine. Miss Strutt was a very religious lady and may even have been a Christian, because she actually demonstrated a trusting faith in God and a missionary zeal towards us little ones without exceeding her tutorial duties. She had many stories to tell to which we listened with great interest. One which particularly impressed me was about her Guardian Angel who, on one occasion, advised her to alter her customary route to school. She always rode to the school on her bicycle from Court Lane in Dulwich where she lived but on the day of visitation a bomb fell in the road where she might otherwise have been. We believed her absolutely, why not, for she had undoubtedly been saved!

She encouraged us to pray and gave me a small card with prayers written on it, which I diligently used although the prayers were for things beyond my understanding. However, she also told us that we could pray anywhere at any time. For many years I mused on that before I discovered the truth of it! Miss Strutt also told us Bible stories in a very interesting way. On one occasion she serialised the story of Joseph. I thought it was wonderful and wanted a copy of the story to read for myself. I had no Bible at home and told my teacher of my need. She said that if I would go to Sunday School each week she would give me a stamp to

stick on a card. When the card was full, she would see if she could find a Bible for me. Miss Strutt also taught a Sunday School class in the school on Sunday afternoons. It must be difficult to match that kind of devotion today, but I did not attend St John's Sunday School. Instead, I went to the hall at the back of Dulwich Grove Congregational Church with my friends. I collected all the stamps and duly received my Bible ... but oh, the disappointment! It was a New Testament and though I searched, the story of Joseph was not in it! Soon afterwards my parents bought a Bible for me. I still have it and it is inscribed 'To Vera, on her ninth birthday, with love from mummy and daddy'. A heavenly Father became very real to me in my childish innocence. Family cares often drove me to pray and though I prayed with such a small amount of faith, all of my tiny petitions were granted and my fears were proved to be so unnecessary.

Vera Conway, 1989

Fell In Stream

In due course, it was time to take my eleven plus, which I passed to go to Honor Oak Grammar School for girls. I enjoyed being there very much. The school was wonderful. It had grass lawns, which were marvellous compared with the playground of Heber Road School. It also had a little stream which separated the junior lawn from the senior lawn. All first formers fell in once. It contained only about three inches of water but we got very wet. I walked to school from Barry Road; it seemed a really long way. We wore navy serge skirts, sky blue shirts, a navy tie with a green stripe, a navy blazer and a beret.

I was in Rowan House. I loved maths and was good at it; I was also good at sport.

Unfortunately, since my older sister was now at work, I was the eldest at home and had to go straight back after school to get the tea for my brothers and sister and then cook the meal for my parents and my older sister. Then I had to do my homework and help with the ironing. On Saturdays I cleaned the flat and got the weekend shopping.

Sheila Davidson, 2001

Cure For Spitting

I have several memories of my last class in St John's Infants School. Our desks were in three columns with the pupils sitting two to each desk with their back towards the North Cross Road end of the room. There was very little space for movement let alone for equipment, so it was not surprising that we sat in our desks all the time and left them only when we were summoned to Mrs Edwards' desk to receive her attention. The little equipment which was found to be necessary was kept on the shelves along the left-hand side of the room. There were kept our blackboards in chalky dust piles, a few books of poor quality paper compared with the beautiful productions which children use nowadays, the thick round pencils and the halves of exercise books, cut for economy. The class reading books were kept there too. Group reading was in vogue and Ginn provided the scheme in its Beacon books. I had learnt to read at an early age with the help of my father, from the *Japhet Annual* which was my only book, so I took Old Lob and his companions in my stride. My reading experience was supplemented outside school by a literary diet of *Dandy* and *Beano* bought for me by my grandparents each week.

The walls of the classrooms were almost bare. Only rarely was any good work pinned up, but reproductions of classical paintings decorated the rooms here and there. To the right of the windows facing us was a small shelf, high up out of our reach. On this shelf rested a jar full of teaspoons, each one recognisable to its owner by some distinguishing mark – the pattern in the metal, for instance, or more commonly, a length of coloured wool round the handle. As the latter never really came clean in its daily cold water bath, a fishy smell dwelt in the jar with the spoons, but it would have taken more than that to put us off our daily dose of cod liver oil and malt! It may even have been that the odour from the jar added to the characteristic smell of the classroom which I know I found distasteful in those days.

Fifty years ago, paper handkerchiefs were unheard of and dirty noses were deplored, so we were all required to bring a handkerchief from home. A daily inspection took place, with us children standing in the aisles between our desks holding up our hankies for Mrs Edwards to see. Some of us, perhaps those of more careless reputation, wore our hankies pinned to our jumpers or gymslips to prevent their loss, for hankies were valuable and comparatively expensive to buy. The poorer families who could not afford the real thing used pieces of rag or torn up sheet ... and sheets had to be positively exhausted before they were torn up to be hankies! However, anything was better than 'cuffing it'.

It was while I was a pupil in this classroom that I learned to cure children of the heinous sin of spitting! Even more emphasis was laid in those days on not spitting than is laid on not smoking today and 'Please do not spit' notices were displayed in all public places including public transport vehicles. Since the tuberculosis bacterium could be spread in that way, spitting was not only unsociable but was also a dangerous practice. One day a boy was hauled in from

Miss Carpenter with her class at St John's School, *c.* 1948.

playtime accused of having spat at another child. He was ordered to take the metal pail (each classroom had one; at lunchtimes the pails were used to deliver warm water to the teachers who used to wash their hands) and to half fill it with water from the washroom. When the boy and the pail were in position behind the blackboard, he was told to continue spitting into the bucket until it was full. My seat at that time was near the front of the column by the door, not far from the blackboard and easel. As the next lesson proceeded, I kept glancing behind to see how he was progressing. He didn't spit once into the pail and no doubt he never spat again in his whole life!

Vera Conway, 1989

Teacher Pulled Knitting Undone

I enjoyed my first year at school – Goodrich Road Infants. I remember the chart on the wall and chanting the sounds 'a' for apple, 'b' for bat etc. We had little blackboards and pieces of chalk.

One teacher I had later liked me as little as I liked her. She frequently pulled my knitting undone even though I had learnt to knit before I had started school. I think we were all glad when this teacher was away and we had a plump, jolly teacher whose name, I think, was Custance, but most of us thought it was Custards.

Brenda Pooley, 2001

How Naughty!

I remember one day when I fell victim to my teacher's wrath. Generally speaking, we were good in those days and naughtiness was more often born of ignorance than of stubbornness or disobedience. My father taught me to knit and I proudly took my efforts to school, not so much to show my teacher, but in the hope of continuing my striped 'knit one, drop one', pattern during the playtime, for having (almost) mastered the skill I was determined to practise it irrespective of what the rest of the world was doing. My mother warned Mrs Edwards about the contents of my bag, suggesting that the needles might be dangerous in the playground, unsupervised! However, I spent playtime knitting, as I had planned and it was not until we lined up to go back into the classroom that Mrs Edwards discovered that I had slipped through the net! For my enthusiasm I earned the title, 'naughty little girl' but the experience taught me something useful for my career with young children.

Behind Mrs Edwards's table was a door which led into Mrs Hahn's room. Mrs Hahn was a tall, grey-haired lady, the kindly wife of the gentleman who later became chief librarian for Camberwell. As Mrs Hahn's duties seemed mainly concerned with the slower children, I was never in her class, but her speciality was music, so on certain occasions Mrs Edwards' class would squash in with hers for 'band'. We beat our instruments to 'Here comes Mrs Macaroni' or 'When Johnny comes marching home again, hurrah, hurrah.' I was almost always given a triangle to play, because there were more triangles than any other instrument and the drums were kept mainly for the boys. So far as I can remember, my yearning to play a drum was never satisfied.

Vera Conway, 1989

Headmaster Used Cane

Our mother took us down to Grove Vale School from our home in Chesterfield Grove

A class at Friern Secondary Girls' School, 1950.

Mr Anderson, headmaster, stands next to the door in a Grove Vale School classroom, 1932.

because East Dulwich Grove was much too dangerous to cross even in the 1930s.

The classrooms went up in steps. Fortunately, I was in the back row for I was a chatterbox and my name was put in the back of the punishment book just once, probably for talking in class. Very serious misdemeanours were dealt with in front of the whole school by the headmaster with a cane.

A teacher played the piano as we went into assembly each morning. I remember *Country Gardens* and other Percy Grainger items.

Christine Brock, 2001

Heber School Remembered

I attended Heber School, a large Victorian building. I remember there being two entrances and two separate playgrounds, one for boys and one for girls. I also remember the outdoor toilet block which always seemed to be freezing cold and I tried to avoid going there.

My sister Vera had taken her 11 plus examination in Wales but when we came back to London the authorities refused to accept her pass and she had to attend a secondary modern school. She was furious as she was a bright girl. She became head girl of Friern Secondary Modern School. Her first job was as a private secretary, today a PA, to Mr Freebody of Debenham and Freebody. In those days everyone worked on Saturdays until lunchtime and it was a great treat that she was allowed to take me with her sometimes.

I remember Heber Road School with affection. I too was quite bright and loved maths, which meant that the teachers liked me and helped me. Mrs Sanderson was my teacher; I thought she was wonderful. I also remember being in a classroom, upstairs somewhere. Our desks stood on a series of broad steps going higher at the back of the class, designed I assume so that all the pupils could see the teacher. We had gas lighting, and our desks were really Victorian with a hole for the porcelain ink wells and a lid which lifted. We kept our books inside and had a seat which was a bench with a plank

Grove Vale School pupils in the playground, *c*. 1935.

A boys' class in Grove Vale School assembled for this photograph, *c*. 1922.

Miss Bonnette's class enjoyed a Christmas party at Dog Kennel Hill School in 1949. Gillian Hiemer (now Johnson-Flint) is on the top row next to the boy on the far left.

of wood at the back, all attached to the desk. I remember being ink monitor which meant holding a wooden tray in which were holes into which one put the porcelain ink wells. I mixed up the ink powder with water and put some in each pot. There was also a milk monitor who pressed through the little card circle in the card lid of the milk bottle and put in a straw ready for playtime. The milk bottle was quite short, squat with a wide mouth in which was a wide circle of card with a hole for the straw. The bottles held a third of a pint of milk.

I remember taking into school a jam jar to collect chocolate powder, probably some Government hand-out. It was delicious, unlike the malt which we were also given. I also remember May Day when we all wore our pretty dresses with flowers and danced round the maypole. On Empire Day

we dressed in red, white and blue and sang patriotic songs.

Sheila Davidson (née Gardiner), 2001

Robber in Play

My son Geoffrey, who was born on 14 August 1944, attended Grove Vale School. At the age of six he was chosen to appear in a school play. He was to be a robber, he told me proudly. I understood it was a fairy tale type of play.

I found some old dark green blackout curtains left over from the war. I made a tunic, cutting the hem and armholes into a deep fringe. A pair of leggings came next. Gold braid ribbon was twisted criss-cross around his legs. A wonderful turban finished it off, complete with a long gold coloured dress clip fastened down the front. He was a fairy tale robber indeed, straight out of Aladdin.

We then visited J. Rogers & Sons, conjuring trick masters at No. 52 Grove Vale, which was known as the joke shop. Here we bought a small black beard and moustache. Geoffrey's male teacher was really delighted with the whole effect. Unfortunately, the other two robbers arrived dressed in their fathers' old caps and mufflers brandishing a toy gun. No one appeared to notice. It was all part of the play which was a great success.

Grace Smith-Grogan, 2001

Dog Kennel Hill School Remembered

My main memories of East Dulwich centre around Dog Kennel Hill (junior mixed) School, which I attended from September 1948 to July 1955. The photograph of my first Christmas party there shows most of my classmates in fancy dress, but for some reason I just wore my party dress. (I'm the one kneeling in the middle with my thumb in my mouth!) I remember some of their names, especially Susan Hoy (the bright-eyed girl at the back) with whom I regained contact seven years ago and David Pawley (the clown seated at the front) who lived next door to me in Camberwell Grove. It would be good to hear from any of them now, to discover how life has treated them.

In January 1949, my lifelong friend Gillian Hiemer (now Mrs Johnson-Flint) joined the school. She has provided a photograph of the Christmas party of that year, when we both attended as fairies. I have a special recollection of the teacher showing this picture to us, trying to identify the boy sitting by the radiator. To my knowledge, we never solved the mystery and thought he must have been a ghost!

For the school years 1951 to 1953 Gillian and I were in Mr Deady's class. Ah yes, Mr Deady! Mr Deady taught us 'joined

Boys from class 4A at Dog Kennel Hill School assembled on the steps in 1955.

Christmas 1948 was a happy occasion at Dog Kennel Hill School.

up' writing. Mr Deady composed stories incorporating our surnames and at the point of inclusion we could leave for home. Mr Deady was never wrong! That was until he taught us that Henry VIII had eight wives. This was hotly disputed by my history-loving mother who wrote down the names of his six wives and demanded to know the other two. Of course, Mr Deady had to admit defeat and things were never quite the same again!

Our final two years at Dog Kennel Hill School were under the beady eye of Miss Oxford, a very strict teacher of the 'old school'. However, when she set us to read quietly on our own, while she concentrated on some other work which took her attention she did seem oblivious to the fact that several of her pupils were slipping away from their seats, crawling around the floor and lining up behind a large cupboard in the same room! During these sessions we would also take paper bags of cocoa and sugar to eat with a moistened finger! As my final report shows, the present-day complaints about large classes are nothing new. Miss Oxford was responsible for forty-five girls and boys.

When we were old enough, Gillian and I would walk down Dog Kennel Hill to the junior public library. The return journey would usually take us through the flats where we would stop off at a sweet shop to spend some of our pocket money on sherbet dips, flying saucers, gob-stoppers, blackjacks and the like.

Sometimes my parents would take me to Dulwich Hamlet Football Club. I remember their shirts of pink and blue squares and being lifted over the turnstiles to avoid the entrance fee! My mother's favourite player was Tommy Jover, a small bald-headed man who played at No. 11 and ran like crazy! On one occasion their opponents were

Miss Bonnette's class at Dog Kennel Hill School during the summer of 1949.

Girls from class 4a at Dog Kennel Hill, July 1955.

an African team who played barefoot. I wonder what they would recall about their time in East Dulwich. Happy days!

Susan Watson (née Loveland), Dover, 2000

Attended Dog Kennel Hill School

I attended Dog Kennel Hill School which was built in 1938 but closed for most of the Second World War. It reopened in 1943.

The playground seemed enormous compared with some Victorian schools in London. The infants' classrooms all opened on to three sides of the playground so that we could go outside to paint at easels – which I still like doing now when I have spare moments.

There were only two floors, with the juniors upstairs, until 'the bulge' when more children who were born in abundance at the end of the war had to be accommodated. A few extra out-buildings were put up quickly and still survive.

Various special days of celebration still stick in my mind. On Commonwealth Day we were allowed to bring Union Flags on sticks to wave, as we skipped around the outside walls of the building after school assembly with hymns and prayers in the morning. My mother said she did something similar for Empire Day when she was young in the early 1920s.

After school I remember being taken to Grove Vale Library with a friend and her mother, soon after it opened in 1950. We could choose books to read other than school reading books which I learnt off by heart especially by the 'Look and Say' method.

As I had lived on the Dog Kennel Hill Estate, it seemed fun to walk back through it to my home in Camberwell Grove – especially as we could visit a sweet shop on the way for ½d or 1d sweets, nuts or a lolly.

When Bessemer Grange Library was newly opened when I was about ten, it was worth walking all that way to find more new books and even the latest Enid Blyton Famous Five volume.

When it was the Coronation time of our Queen, there was great celebration. As a school we were lined up along the upper part of Denmark Hill to wave to the Queen in her car as she drove past much too fast, I thought, to see her properly. But it was some solace to be given a special commemorative pen and propelling pencil set afterwards at the school. It was royal blue with gold lettering on it.

Gillian Johnson-Flint, 2000

Last Day at School

My last day at Adys Road School was very happy. We played netball against another school and we won, and my teacher gave me a green shamrock brooch in a box. I put it under my pillow that night and cried myself to sleep, as I was sorry to leave school and feared what the future had for me, but that is another story.

Elsie Stukings, 1976

A class at Adys Road School, *c.* 1933. Mr Way, the headmaster, is on the left with a class teacher, Mr Robinson, on the right.

CHAPTER 4

Commerce

A number of butchers shops closed in East Dulwich after Sainsbury's opened a store on Dog Kennel Hill in 1992. This picture of Redgewell's at No. 38 Lordship Lane is a reminder of a popular butchers shop in an era before superstores caused the closure of many local shops.

Thriving Shopping Centre

It is interesting to walk along Memory Lane and remember the shops along Lordship Lane after the Second World War. Starting where the roundabout was created at Goose Green after the tramlines were removed, on the right was Samuel Gates, newsagent; the premises are still used for the same purpose. On the left at No. 5 was a record and music shop under the name of Follet. The shop sold 78rpm records and later LPs and 45rpm. The first long playing record I bought there was the music from *Oklahoma*. Next door was Stanley Dew, tobacconist.

Next to where Chener Books is today was

The Foresters Arms, Lordship Lane.

a lending library. Crossing the road to No. 23, one came to Batley's grocer's with whom our family was registered with our ration books. This is now an estate agent.

A public house, The Foresters Arms, was on the corner of Crawthew Grove. Crossing this side turning, one arrives at No. 29 Lordship Lane which was White's photographic studios. This was run by George and Dorothy White; George's hobby was magic. He appeared as 'Mr Ree' in hospitals, children's parties and any other group who showed interest. In the age when records were 78rpm, he and his wife would go to St Francis Hospital on a Sunday to play requests for the old patients. When the lease on No. 29 expired, George White moved to a shop on the corner of North Cross Road and Ulverscroft Road. He still did photography but he concentrated on selling art materials. He and his wife then retired to a flat on a Peabody Estate in Deptford. George died in an old people's home in Bromley aged ninety-three.

Opposite George White's shop in Lordship Lane were two small shops – one a tobacconist's named Blewett; the other was a jeweller's. Next door at No. 32 was a hardware store named Walter's; Dulwich DIY provides an excellent service there today. Also on that parade between East Dulwich Grove and Matham Grove were a butcher's, electrical shop, ladies' hair salon and a fish and chip shop on the corner called Perfecto.

Crossing to the left-hand side, a Woolworths was built where George White's shop and three others were. The Social Security office is on the site today. Further along were Brewster's Men's Wear and A.H. Wheeler's, who had two shops. Number 41 was for storage of trestle tables and other items for wedding receptions. The shop on the corner of Frogley Road was Wheeler's baker's with the bakery behind; this is now used as a car repair shop.

When my family moved into the area, in the yard behind No. 41 Lordship Lane there were barrows which had been used to transport the bread to their other shops in East Dulwich Road and Dulwich Village. These were replaced by an Austin Seven van. Crossing to the right-hand side, there was, and still is, a chemist's on the corner of Matham Grove. Next to it was an off-licence – as today. The last shop on that parade was Wybrow's electrical repair shop where one could get accumulators recharged for the old kind of radio. From this shop to the bank on the corner of Ashbourne Grove was a small row of houses where Somerfield is today.*

Peter Morris, 2001

*It is now a Co-operative food store which opened on 25 March 2010.

We Shopped Close to Home

When I was a child we lived in Gowlett Road, SE15, but at the top of the road was East Dulwich Road, SE22. I remember the shops which still exist between the Goose Green playground and Gowlett Road and are now being smartened up as part of the Bellenden renewal area scheme.

On the corner was a second-hand furniture shop. Next to that was a chemist's with a post office counter. The chemist was a Scotsman who always wore a white coat as did the young lady who assisted him. I used to go to the post counter a lot because I had a Post Office Savings book and used to save

the money I earned from my paper round and money given as birthday presents.

The newsagent I worked for was next door. I delivered papers in the morning and evening. The shop also sold sweets and delicious custard ice cream which was put on to a cone with a wooden spoon. The next shop had windows painted over; it was a wholesale haberdasher's. There was a lovely old-fashioned dairy. The milk roundsman pushed a three-wheeled milk cart.

Also in the block of shops was a butcher's and a fish and chip shop. I remember how excited we were when it opened because we had never bought fish and chips from a shop where you could slosh vinegar and salt on from big containers on the counter. There were also big jars of pickled onions. My mother would send us for four pieces of cod at 3d each and 4d worth of chips – 1s 4d for a good meal for four of us.

Then there was Mr Leach's oil shop where we took the accumulators to be charged for our wireless set. We also went there for vinegar which was poured from a barrel into our own bottle. The shop supplied us with paraffin for our Valor oil stove which was used to heat the kitchen before we came downstairs for breakfast. Mr Leach wore a brown overall and Mrs Leach sometimes helped in the shop. They had two daughters, Joan and Daphne, and a son, Basil, who became a councillor in Bellenden Ward and was active at St John the Evangelist Church.

Also in the terrace of shops was a grocer's shop where my mother was given a chair to sit on while she placed her order. The shop had a bacon slicing machine; we always had back rashers cut to No. 8 thickness.

Next door was a cake and bread shop. After we had been swimming at Dulwich Baths we used to go there to buy ½ lb of stale cakes. The shop next to that was a stationer's which also did printing. I could hear the steam engine that worked the printing press. The noise always seemed to be in the background when we were playing on Goose Green.

Derek Austin, 2001

Mini Harrods called Trundle's

I did most of the shopping for my mum at Hammett's (butcher's), Penfold's (greengrocer's and florist's), David Greig (grocer's), Mr Hunt's and Mr Paul's (sweets, cigarettes, newspapers etc). We even had a 'mini Harrods' called Trundle's. It was a fairly small shop in comparison with the Knightsbridge store but it did have its own departments.

My friend's mum had a café called Pat's Café. There were also Lockhart's (toys and stationery), Pullin's (motorbikes), a post office and a bank on each corner of Ashbourne Grove, hence nicknamed 'the river' by us kids.

Joyce Woods (née Mason), 2000

Hats were Fashionable

I can visualise two little girls comparing their best Sunday hats. 'Mine cost 3s 1d', said one proudly. 'Mine cost 4s 11d', boasted the other. The first child couldn't believe it so walked all the way to Trundle's department store at Nos. 69-75 Lordship Lane to find out, by inspecting the pretty lacy summer straw hats decorating the window each on its own little stand.

How I miss the hat shops with their attractive designs! Will hats ever come back into fashion again I wonder?

Grace Smith-Grogan, 2000
(aged eighty-one)

What a Lot of Shops and Stalls!

Prior to the Second World War, Lordship Lane was a thriving, busy 'High Street'. It had three pubs; various greengrocers, butchers, grocers, men's outfitters, boot and shoe sales and repair shops (Brown's and Frewin's); two toy shops (The Dorothy Bazaar and Lockhart's); a shop which sold records, sheet music and a few musical instruments (Follett's); two tobacconists; two or three sweetshops and many others including Trundle's Department Store which occupied four shops opposite Ashbourne Grove. This emporium sold household linens, dress fabrics, ladies', children's and babies' clothes and also had a ladies' hat department. Lordship Lane boasted two hardware/ironmonger's shops, Walter's (still going strong as Dulwich DIY and run by a very efficient Indian family), and Shinkfield's which occupied two shops where the video shop is now, opposite the post office. Shinkfield's had at one time belonged to a firm called Hutchison's which did furniture removals. They stabled their horses and pantechnicon in the yard which runs behind the Lord Palmerston and the adjoining shops, with access from North Cross Road. The pantechnicon and horses were housed in a large building which backed onto No. 57 Nutfield Road, where I was born and where I lived until 1966 when I moved to No. 60.

Lordship Lane also had two branches of the David Greig organisation and Le Chardon restaurant, which occupies one of the two shops, still has the 'thistle' tiles in its decor. The Maypole, United Dairies, the Home & Colonial and the Co-op all provided groceries and provisions as did a super shop owned by Mr and Mrs Killinger, who sold tea and coffee from large 'Ali Baba' type canisters. Sugar and dried fruit were weighed into blue paper bags. I wanted

Mrs Edna Edgar and her daughter Christine walking along Lordship Lane with John Edgar in his pram around 1933. The Co-op, which was bombed in 1944, is across the road.

to work in this lovely shop when I grew up, although the temptation to cut, pat and stamp butter in David Greig's was a great rival for my affections.

On the west side of Lordship Lane, between East Dulwich Grove and Matham Grove, was a gent's outfitters (J.K. Wallace). At some time in the 1950s or '60s, when the shop was being adapted for other purposes, one of the workmen was frightened by the appearance of an old man with a grey beard whom he met on the stairs. This was reported in the *South London Observer* and when my mother read about it, she said 'Oh that must be the ghost of old Mr Wallace'. She had known him when she was a girl and lived in Crawthew Grove.

We also had two lending libraries, one in Templeman's, a high class stationer's. At No. 52 Lordship Lane there was a radio shop, Wybrow's, where we took the accumulator for our battery-operated wireless to be charged each week for 6d.

Unlike today, there were no restaurants at all – hard to believe – but Wheeler's the baker's with one of their shops and the bakehouse on the corner of Frogley Road, did have a tea shop next door.

We had bakers and bakehouses all over the place then. Hemmings' had a shop and bakehouse on the corner of Bawdale Road. This was next to the other David Greig shop and North Cross Road had two shops belonging to Hurst's the baker's, their premises and bakehouse being on the corner of Fellbrigg Road and at the junction with Crystal Palace Road. All these bakeries provided good freshly baked bread and cakes – not a cut, wrapped loaf in sight.

Off Lordship Lane in Shawbury Road, just behind the then United Dairies, was a farrier's. What a joy it was to watch the horses being shod; I can still recall the sharp smell of burning hoof as the shoes were being fitted.

Also in Shawbury Road and next door to the farrier's was a Salvation Army hall, where as children we could watch 'improving' films for free.

Also off Lordship Lane was another busy street market – North Cross Road. This street was lined on the south side with shops and stalls, some being extensions of the shops themselves. These included flower stalls, a sweet stall, cats' meat stall and 'Bookie's', where one could exchange books and comics either for free or for a small price, ½d or 1d. There was also a store which sold nothing but rabbits (dead ones, of course). The provision shops like Wheatley's and Cook's sold hearthstone, carbolic soap, etc. from the stalls in the gutter, away from the food. When I recall all the various butchers, greengrocers and many other shops and look at it now, a rather dreary street given over almost entirely to shops converted into houses, it is rather sad. We had a wet and fried fish shop (Pocock's) where the electricity sub-station is, and one could select a fish in the front part of the shop and have it cooked in the back part to take home all fresh and appetising. There were at least three butchers. One of them,

Eric Smith's greengrocer's shop at No. 21 Lordship Lane, which he took over in December 1960, is now run by his son Dave, seen here in 1967. The shop has been a greengrocer's since the early twentieth century.

Gilbert's, opposite the then St John's School, also opened in the evenings to sell saveloys, pease pudding, faggots, pigs' trotters and boiled bacon all hot – oh, the mouth watering smells! At No. 53 North Cross Road, Mr and Mrs Howard had a dairy which sold milk from a large china swan and the milk was ladled into your jug. I suppose they did sell milk in bottles, but I do not remember them.

Instead of launderettes, in the 1930s there were a number of laundry receiving offices where dirty linen could be taken, either for the 'bag wash' (a cheap version of laundry which one had to collect all wet and tangled up in a bag) or, if you could afford it, the washing could be fully finished, i.e. dried and ironed. The laundries were behind the shop between North Cross Road and Shawbury Road and the East Dulwich Steam Laundry on the corner of Bassano Street.

Stella Baker, 2000

Shopped in the Co-op

We used to shop locally; there were no supermarkets in those days. We did our weekly shop in the Co-op in Crystal Palace Road. It had long counters of dark polished wood and behind the counter at the back were marble slabs on which butter, margarine, lard, bacon, cheese and eggs were kept. I think the marble helped to keep it cool. The cheese, butter, margarine and lard were in huge blocks which were cut off to the size you wanted. Sugar was in a huge bag which was spooned out into smaller bags which had a blue paper liner. Biscuits were in large tins with glass lids and these would be weighed into bags. The Co-op used to sell broken biscuits cheaply which was a godsend to a large family with little money. Next door was the butcher – again the Co-op. When we bought

anything we were given a little piece of paper receipt, which we took to the cashier who then exchanged it for tokens made of tin, of various denominations. These were collected and sorted into one pound piles. Each one was wrapped in newspaper. Once a year these were taken back to the Co-op and exchanged for money.

Day to day, we shopped just round the corner in Goodrich Road and Landells Road at a family-run greengrocer's. On the next corner, Goodrich Road and Crystal Palace Road, was a grocer where we bought odd things but it was more expensive than the Co-op. I remember going for broken biscuits and was made to feel a fool because his biscuits were whole and more expensive. Across the corner was a baker who made wonderful rolls, cream slices and doughnuts. My sister, brothers and I used to swim in Dulwich Baths regularly and would walk back up Crystal Palace Road, buy a roll and some chips from across the road, stuff the chips inside the roll and sit with our backs to the grille in front of the baker's shop which was hot because of the heat coming from the bakery under the shop. It helped to dry us as somehow we were never able really to dry ourselves after swimming. Amazingly, much later one of my daughters lived in a flat above the baker's and now one of my nephews lives in the same flat.

We often went to Rye Lane to shop for clothes or fabrics. My sister and I used to make our own clothes and often walked from Barry Road to Jones and Higgins in the morning, bought our own fabric, walked back home, made the dress in the afternoon and wore it in the evening.

For shoes we went to a shop in Lordship Lane. It had long counters in mahogany and a system of a series of pulleys to send the money to the cashier who sat in a little cubicle raised from the floor, in one corner. The assistant put the money in a container like a large bullet, twisted it to close it, then put it in a container over the counter which transported it along the wires to the cashier.

It was difficult for my mother to feed and clothe us all, so she belonged to a club paying a certain amount each week and after a while would get a 'cheque' which she could then spend in this shop to buy us clothes and shoes. My father was a builder all his life. It was hard for him to find work and he often went away to work. It seemed that all my childhood I didn't see my father very much.

Our milk was delivered by George the milkman with his horse and trolley with rubber wheels. Two brothers were our window cleaners who came on their bicycles with ladders. A rag and bone man used to come along with his horse and cart and called out something which we interpreted as 'jerombe', but goodness knows what he called. We all used to run out to see him and his horse.

Sheila Davidson, 2001

Stalls Lit with Naphtha

The North Cross Road street market was lit at night with naphtha flares. Mothers shopped there on Saturday nights when goods were cheapest.

One of my earliest memories is of standing on Titus Ward's corner (No. 45) in tears because I couldn't see my Mummy. She appeared from just around the corner immediately but I still remember the desolated feelings.

Christine Brock, 2001

Bought Sticky Buns

On my way to school I would buy sticky fruit buns from the baker's on the corner of North Cross Road and Fellbrigg Road. We got two

for a penny. My weekly pocket money was a threepenny bit which was a lot in those days.

Joyce Woods (née Mason), 2000

Biscuits sold Loose

My aunt was the cashier at Gosling's, the grocer's on the corner of Crebor Street and Dunstans Road. When Mr Gosling went on holiday, she was left in charge, and I remember her taking me round the back of the shop.

Biscuits were mostly loose in tins and weighed out as customers wanted them. Sugar was weighed onto squares of blue paper which were then folded into packets. Other dry goods were tipped into cones made out of a sheet of paper. Milk was sold in cartons from Blade's Dairy.

Brenda Pooley, 2001

Served well in Small Shops

Before the Second World War, East Dulwich Road, Upland Road and North Cross Road had many small shops. These were well supported by local people who were always served well and pleasantly.

Elsie Blenkey, 2000

Shop was Child's Delight

I used to run errands for a lady who lived next door to the present vicarage. In those days the vicarage was called Walnut Tree Villa. The lady always gave me a penny. I would go either to the toy shop in Grove Vale which was like a Dickens' shop with very thick bow-shaped windows. When you entered, a bell used to clang. You went down one step into a gloomy shop, but it was a child's delight. We took our time spending our penny, as there were china dolls no bigger than one's thumb, glass beads and glass marbles, five-stones, tops and pink-iced mice, and a host of other toys. Or I would go to Piper's, a grocer's shop in Lordship Lane, and ask for broken biscuits. The man would make a newspaper cone and fill it with broken biscuits. We would wet two fingers and eat them on the way home and then sit down to a big dinner. What a greedy girl!

Elsie Stukings, 1976

Props Made for Magicians

Rennie Honour has owned the shop at No. 52 Grove Vale for about twenty years. Before that it was Chener Books and years ago it was a joke shop.*

We had a visitor who told us that it was his grandfather who had run the joke shop. The back of the shop was then the family parlour; the old man used to sit there by the fire, eating kippers. As a treat, his children (our informant's mother, aunts and uncles) were allowed to suck the kipper bones. This gentleman also made props for magicians. As one of his daughters had particularly strong, dark hair which could be used for invisible threads in these devices, she was not allowed to leave home until of quite advanced age! I am glad to say the shop shows no signs of being haunted.

The top of the ash tree in the back garden was blown off by a bomb during the Blitz.

Jon Gunson, 2001

*It is now Blackbird Bakery.

Collars taken to be Laundered

My mother sent my sister aged ten, accompanied by me when I was only three, to a laundry receiving office in Grove Vale where we left our father's stiff collars to be laundered. It was such a long walk for tired little legs. We then had to go back to collect the shining white starched collars in a crisp paper bag which we carried home very carefully.

There was also a joke shop in Grove Vale where children bought itching powder and sneezing powder – and also small pink caps for toy guns.

Grace Smith-Grogan, 2000

Off-licences in Back Streets

The Edenberg at No. 82 Crawthew Grove was an off-licence. There were others on the corners of back streets off Lordship Lane until thirty to forty years ago. I remember especially that on the two corners of Landells Road by Goodrich Road there was the Surrey Arms on one side and the Kentish Arms on the other – showing that the boundary of the two counties was nearby.

Kathleen Davis, 2001

Street Activity

Early memories I have are of watching the lamp-lighter working his way along the road; the muffin man with a tray on his head and ringing a bell, baker's and milkmen's horses and the rag and bone men with a barrow or horse and cart.

Christine Brock, 2001

Fed Stale Buns to Elephants

My sister Valerie and I remember two old ladies, who were probably twins, who lived in Oakhurst Grove. They always dressed in Victorian clothes and carried parasols in the summer.

Then there was 'Uncle Fred' who had a Wall's ice cream cart in the summer; he would cut a snowfruit in half so that it cost only ½d instead of 1d. In the winter he came round on Sunday afternoons with a tray on his head with crumpets and muffins; he used to ring a handbell.

When we were being taken to the zoo, which was quite often, we would go to Wheeler's baker's shop in East Dulwich to buy a bag of stale buns to give to the elephants.

Because there were cobble stones around the tramlines in East Dulwich Road I often saw horses pulling coal carts slip on the wet cobble stones. They had to be unharnessed to allow them to stand up again. I once witnessed an awful accident when a coal cart came out of Oakhurst Grove and the horse could not stop. Its head went through the window of a tram. The poor creature was very badly cut. With its head wrapped in blankets, it was walked up Crystal Palace Road to East Dulwich Police Station where it died in the yard. It made me feel so ill that I could not go back to school that afternoon.

Derek Austin, 2001

Helped on Milk Round

Father had a milk round in East Dulwich and a horse called Peggy. By the time I was about ten or eleven years of age I would go with him on the round, strictly against the local bye-laws, and help with the deliveries or ride on the iron-tyred milk float.

Frank Staples in *Fifty Years In The Milk Game*, 1996

Watched Laundry Furnace

We would often stop to talk to Bill who stoked the furnace which heated the water for the laundry on the corner of Bassano Street. In winter we would linger in the warm glow of the great fire, but his task was unenviable in summer! We would watch him stoking the flames with shovels full of coal and we could see deep into the white heat of the blazing fuel. We needed little imagination to help us to understand the trials of Shadrach, Meshach and Abednego! Hell fire to us meant Bill's furnace.

If the laundry door was open, as it often was if the weather was fine, we could stand and watch the women working inside, feeding the sheets through the mangle and watching them emerge all white and smooth and ready to be folded. Gran had worked on a mangle in a laundry when she was young and would often exchange a cheery word with these girls with whom she felt an affinity.

Vera Conway, 2001

Watched Blacksmith

A blacksmith had a forge next to the Salvation Army hall in Shawbury Road and I remember watching him working. With the disappearance of horses, he continued by making ornamental ironwork.

On the opposite side of the road, where the entrance to flats is now, was a very gloomy shop used by a cobbler. I think it probably closed before the Second World War.

Kathleen Pickard, 2000

Food Bought Daily

Shopping was an important part of the daily routine for our mothers and grandmothers – and for us too when we were not at school. In the days before domestic refrigerators and when storage space was limited, a daily trip to the shops was a necessity. The little money we had was eked out for those things which we could not do without, mainly food.

'Give us this day our daily bread' was fully significant to us. We got to know the shops which we frequented very well; we also got to know our neighbours well because we met them so often in the shops. The little corner shops, most of which have been closed, demolished or altered, were wonderful places for picking up and passing on all the latest local news. One corner shop in particular featured in our early lives, that which was kept by Mr and Mrs Fenn on the corner where the road bends in Colwell Road. Their lovely cat often sat on the counter (how unhygienic). She had mothered innumerable kittens in her time. The shop was scrupulously clean and tidy and any groceries, sweets or cigarettes could be bought there. The selection was amazing for such a small shop but, of course, there was not so much to choose from as there is nowadays.

Vera Conway, 2001

Naked Encounter

For many years my brother lived in East Dulwich (off Lordship Lane) and was a doorstep insurance agent (a man from the Pru). He had many stories to tell of his experiences with the weekly premiums. Here is one:

On a very warm summer's day he was trudging around his neighbourhood collecting the money. His mid-afternoon call took him to a house where upon knocking the door it was opened by a six-year-old girl who was completely naked and with skin the colour of ebony. Turning round, she called out – 'Momma MAN'. Up the passage came striding her mother also without clothing on and with ebony skin. 'Oh ha', she said. 'Insurance. I go get book and munnie'.

As she retreated down the passage my brother called out to her, 'Lady, when you come back would you mind putting something on'. Shortly afterwards she returned, with the green book and money in her right hand – and wearing a STRAW HAT!

Leonard R. Moncrieff (Canada), 2001

Friday was Fish Day

Next to Lockheart's was Woodall's shoe shop. I remember musing on this often ... why was the proprietor called Mr Fruin, or was he really Mr Woodall? I never found out but he equipped my family and me with all the shoes we ever wore in those days and even supplied the first shoes that my own little son wore. He was quite charming and polite as a shopkeeper and even dealt patiently with my little sister's tantrums when she wanted red fashion shoes rather than the sensible ones chosen for her by my mother. I remember buying my first court shoes from him. 'Will your mother mind you having high heels?' he asked with real concern.

On the corner of Hansler Road was the wet fish shop and Friday was fish day. No one knew why Friday was fish day, but I have no doubt that the fishmonger encouraged the custom. From the sheer habit, mum and gran queued up with all their neighbours to buy cod, skate or plaice for the most economical meal of the week, all served up with a good dollop of parsley. We children stood captivated by the live eels jostling in their metal box and watched while the fishmonger chopped them and the pieces went on moving.

Queues were always so compliant, orderly and fair in those days. I remember one day my gran marched to the front of the queue to greet the friendly fishmonger. She was always unconventional but it was unheard-of behaviour to jump the queue! She was swiftly put in her place.

The shop on the corner of Hansler Road changed hands several times, but I think that it was Marriot's for a while and sold toys and prams. I know for sure that my last doll came from there and I was really far too 'old' to have a baby doll that made its nappy wet when it was fed, but it was plastic and I was charmed by it. My sister and I had one each for Christmas that year.

Vera Conway, 2001

Hats went up in Flames

My memory of the fire in the tropical helmet factory in East Dulwich Road is vivid. I saw the flames curling round the piles of strange white hats. I didn't know the purpose of the hats at the time.

Spectators stood on Goose Green to watch the fire at Vero's in February 1923. As far as I know, nobody was hurt. The firm went on to make industrial hard hats and crash helmets. That fire was symbolic in a way and could be said to forecast the end of colonialism, as District Commissioners wore such hats.

J.G. Morris, 2000

Paper was Scarce

Between David Greig's and the shoe shop was Lockheart's the stationer's. Mr and Mrs Lockheart had two shops. The other, which was further down Lordship Lane, sold mainly toys. They managed both shops themselves until later they received some help from their son and their daughter, Marjorie. Sadly, the son died at an early age, but Marjorie was still loyally helping in the shop years later, when I returned home from college. Her small son was often put outside the shop in his pram to sleep. Imagine how surprised I was to find him a Deacon in East Dulwich Tabernacle when we joined that church in the early 1990s!

Both shops were well stocked and gloriously muddled. They were Aladdin's caves for me. I was especially attracted to the stationery shop and spent most of my pocket money in there. I loved to draw but paper was in very short supply. Even in school we used blackboards for much of the time. My grandfather used to roll his own cigarettes using special Rizla papers and tobacco in a little roller. The tobacco, which always felt damp and smelt lovely, came wrapped in silver paper to keep it fresh. Grandfather would wrap my weekly sixpenny piece and a threepenny piece for my sister in the empty silver paper wrappings. Then I would rush off to Lockheart's and ask for, 'Sixpennyworth of paper please'. I preferred Mrs Lockheart to serve me. She had known me for so long and knew what I wanted. She was more generous and would search around her shop to make up a bundle for me. How precious it was! I hardly dared to use it lest I needed a piece for something more important. Even now that paper is so plentiful and cheap, I cannot bring myself to waste a scrap.

Vera Conway, 2001

Shops used Forecourts

Between Bawdale Road and Hansler Road were several shops which we frequented. All the shops in this row had forecourts and David Greig's made full use of theirs. There was a veritable sea of eggs in shades of brown and white cascading down to the verge of the pavement. They were not sold in nice protective boxes, but placed in brown paper bags, often with a warning from the assistant, 'Mind, yereggseron the top'. It was not unusual to get a bad one either. There were two counters inside the shop and usually there were queues at both of them. The first queue was for the fats and bacon. We children were always fascinated by the bacon slicing machine. It was operated by hand – no electrical equipment in those days – and I can still hear the knife cutting through the meat as the slicer moved backwards and forwards. Cheese was cut to customers' requirements with a wire cutter on a marble slab. Margarine, lard and our tiny bit of butter were weighed and wrapped in greaseproof paper. While all this was going on, we children amused ourselves by making patterns with the sawdust that was sprinkled on the black and white chequered, tiled floor.

Having completed their purchases at the fats counter, mum and gran would move across the shop to the next queue, to buy their groceries. All these foods were rationed, so they had to check that they had enough coupons as well as money to buy what they needed. Everything had to be carefully weighed into brown paper bags. Usually, the bag was placed into the shining brass scale pan and the commodity was measured into the bag using a scoop. We bought tea, sugar, dried fruit (which had to be cleaned and 'picked over' before it could be used), macaroni (for puddings), pudding rice (we never ate rice with a savoury meal), salt, pepper, spices for our bread puddings (nothing was wasted), flour and uninteresting biscuits. I once saw some pictures of bourbon biscuits, custard creams and chocolate biscuits on the side of a tin in a shop, but years were to pass before we tasted such delicacies. Powdered milk and eggs came in large tins as the fresh variety was not always available.

Vera Conway, 2001

Shopped at Co-op

Lordship Lane and North Cross Road were busy shopping areas. As our mother was not in good health, we girls had to do our share of the chores. I used to help my sister do the shopping and we had to adhere strictly to the list prepared by our mother. This list was altered again and again as her housekeeping budget was very limited.

Most of the shopping was done at the Co-op which gave a dividend. We used to collect the tin checks which we used to play shops with, until there were enough to pay into mum's dividend book. The amount saved was spent at the Co-op near the Heaton Arms to buy household goods. I can also remember getting some goods at David Greig's, now a restaurant, and at the Home and Colonial next to the Lord Palmerston. In David Greig's all payments had to be made to the cashier who sat high up in a wooden alcove at the back of the shop – these wooden fittings are still there along with tiled walls and marble shelves where goods were displayed. Meat was always bought at Redgewell's. The old original name plate has recently been discovered over the shop and is used, I am pleased to say, by the present café owners.

I used to queue each Saturday standing on the sawdust-covered tiled floor clutching the

An electric tram passes the Lord Palmerston in Lordship Lane.

ration books for the family. When rationing came we were considered lucky enough to have sufficient points to buy a joint. This was generally a leg or shoulder of lamb, but had to last six of us for four days. It was always roast on Sunday, cold meat and bubble and squeak on Monday (washday), shepherd's pie on Tuesday and stew on Wednesday. If when I returned home the meat was too fat or too large (i.e. too expensive), back I had to go with it. Oh how I dreaded getting the meat!

Gill Harding, 2001

Went Looking for Father

After crossing North Cross Road and passing the Lord Palmerston, the pub on the corner, we came to another wet fish shop and then to Shinkfield's ironmonger's. I always found this shop interesting and welcomed an opportunity to go inside where the many tools and implements were on display. There were gardening tools which I knew that my father would love to have, though a real garden was nothing more than a dream. Washing boards were fairly cheap and prominent and had scrubbing brushes to go with them. I would love a washing board now! There were no brightly coloured plastic things but the new, shiny, galvanised buckets and baths were attractive and longer lasting.

Trundle's came next and second only to Jones and Higgins in Peckham; this was the department store which kept the citizens of East Dulwich in warm underwear and clothing and supplied many of their textile needs. Our liberty bodices with rubber bottoms and our fleecy lined bloomers came from here. One of the delights for children visiting Trundle's was their very effective system for payment. The assistant would place the cash in a little pot which was hanging above our heads. She would then pull a handle to release the pot which travelled along a line to the cash desk. Before long, it would come speeding back with the change and the receipt inside. Delightful! Although we had moved by the time I went away to college, all my trousseau came from the shop, as well as sheets, pillow cases, towels and serviettes. That was in 1955.

My dad was always a problem when he needed new trousers or overalls for his work. He was six feet tall and trousers 'off the peg' ended mid calf on his long legs! For this reason, he would visit Mr Messent who had a shop on the other side of Lordship Lane between Chesterfield and Ashbourne Groves. Umbrella repairs formed an additional part of his trade. Gran had a problem too; she was O.S. This necessitated giving her custom to Knight's shop which catered for larger ladies and sold the sizes that gran needed. Mr Knight was an elderly, bespectacled gentleman and his very prim and proper unmarried daughter worked with him. The shop was scrupulously tidy, with everything kept in a grand system of wooden drawers behind the counter, all carefully labelled. The polished wooden counters had a brass measure along its length and a high stool stood beside it for the use of customers. All the prices seemed to end in 'eleven three', so gran's stockings seemed cheaper at 1s 11 ¾d and not 2s. She always chose silk and lisle and kept them up with suspenders which hung from her corsets. Knight's sold new suspenders, hair ribbons, buttons and the big white

The Royal Arsenal Co-operative Society had a store in Lordship Lane.

A road to Sainsbury's store was made across King's College sports ground in 1991.

handkerchiefs that were luxuries for our men in those days. Pieces of rag were good enough for the rest of us. There were no paper hankies then.

If we ever went further down Lordship Lane than Shinkfield's or Trundle's, it would be to go to the art shop, White's, on the corner of Frogley Road or to the bible bookshop which, later, became the 'Radiant Word Publications', opposite Matham Grove. It always seemed, in my memory, a bit gloomy and not very interesting at the end of the Lane. There was no roundabout there then, only a big junction where the tram points were changed. Follett's record shop sold sheet music and a tiny tobacconist was tucked in somewhere near the public house which is now named the East Dulwich

Tavern. That reminds me of a story.

I remember one day in November 1942 when my mother was still confined to bed after the birth of my sister. Mothers had to spend days in bed in those days so what we would have done without gran, I cannot tell. Grandfather was still working with his son in Bernard Anson's builder's yard in Pellatt Road, so gran had to leave us sometimes to prepare his meals. After she had gone, I stood in the living room, thinking. No doubt, my mother in the next room was wondering what I was up to. A line of clean baby washing was drying on the line that hung over the range. Gran had stoked up the fire and left everything tidy. I had to think what to do next. I decided to go and meet my dad and felt quite sure that I could do this on my own without anyone to accompany me. I turned left out of Bassano Street into Lordship Lane and walked purposefully past the 'Welfare' house where they doled out cod liver oil and powdered milk, past the Working Men's Club, past Kellaway's funeral parlour and past the newsagent's where we bought our *Daily Herald* and where our radio accumulators were left to be recharged. (When I was a little older I carried the accumulators to and from the shop myself. They were made of glass and filled with acid. It was society that was trusted and not just the individual.)

The Chester Café was owned by my friend Sylvia's aunt and uncle who lived next door to the family at No. 20 Bassano Street. I crossed Chesterfield Grove to Wheeler's baker's on the opposite corner and along the pavement as far as Lockheart's toy shop. Mrs Lockheart was standing at her door watching the world go by. 'Where are you going on your own?' she asked. 'I'm going to meet my dad,' I told her confidently. I walked on to Goose Green and, as I had been trained to do, I asked someone to take me across the road. I waited for as long as my patience would allow at the bus stop in East Dulwich Road, just beyond Spurling Road, but my dad did not appear. I thought that I might have missed him, so I went to the tobacconist's near the pub. Sally Dew peered over her till and looked down at me. 'Has my dad been in for his cigarettes yet?' I asked. 'No dear. It's too early for him to come in yet,' she told me.

Yes, it was hours too early. Never mind! I just walked home again – to find my mother quite frantic. At least I proved that at five and a half years of age, I was capable of coping with the big world outside on my own. Dangers in those days came from the incidents of war and seldom from our fellow citizens. We all took care of each other very well.

Vera Conway, 2001

CHAPTER 5

Parks and Public Services

Peckham Rye Park was featured on many postcards in the early twentieth century.

Visited Peckham Rye Park

I recall having a tricycle, red in colour and associated with a Walt Disney character named Mickey Mouse. I rode it to Peckham Rye Park through an alleyway known as Solomon's Passage.

During my childhood I often went to the park where I sometimes watched the bowls. There were brightly coloured flower beds, white doves and the most beautiful peacocks which displayed their tails for the benefit of the peahens. The pond had goldfish in it and nearby were rose arches and the scent in summer was wonderful.

I believe that these experiences helped me to better understand a hymn which I was very fond of – 'All things bright and beautiful.'

Jeffrey Harold Avis, 2000

Happy Times Spent in Park

From the 1920s until the Second World War, Peckham Rye was crowded with families picnicking on Easter Monday, Whit Monday and August Bank Holiday. Latecomers had difficulty in finding a vacant spot. Many families visited Wilson's fair which was held nearby. This was a great attraction and well supported.

Peckham Rye Park was a great joy for everyone. It was beautifully kept and the flowers everywhere were lovely. There were park-keepers and they saw that no damage was done.

There were two cafés – one near the bowling green and another just outside the park. There were many grass tennis courts and two or three hard courts. Apart from the ducks, there were peacocks near the bowling green and these were a great attraction. There was a pond just outside the park where dogs could go for a swim. We used to call it the dog pond. There was a bandstand on the Rye and concerts were given there every Sunday during the summer.

The park was well used by many folk – there were few cars in those days. In the afternoons mothers would bring their children to play on the grass or to go to the playground where there were swings and other activities. At the weekends during the greater part of the year many families visited the park. I have many happy memories of time spent there.

Elsie Blenkey, 2000

Australian Mayor presented a Plant

One memory of Peckham Rye Park goes back to about 1948. I visited the Australian Camberwell Mayor in Melbourne to thank their people for the food parcels sent to the Metropolitan Borough of Camberwell during the Second World War.

I was presented with a myrtle plant by the Mayor which, on my return to London, I

The Visitor Centre in Peckham Rye Park was opened by Councillor Janet Heatley (deputy mayor) on 22 June 1997. She was accompanied by Councillor Niall Duffy, Leader of Southwark Council.

The Peckham Society and the Friends of Peckham Rye Park campaigned for new toilets to be built in the park. Their efforts were successful when derelict public toilets were converted into an attractive Visitor Centre.

The bridge in Peckham Rye Park was a popular feature near the beginning of the twentieth century.

The beautiful Peckham Rye Park during October some time in the early twentieth century.

The spire of St John the Evangelist Church can be seen behind trees on Goose Green.

presented to Peckham Rye Park. For the first few years it was housed in their glasshouses and shown at local horticultural shows. After it had grown considerably, it was planted outside. For many years I used to make an annual visit to watch its progress.

In Camberwell, Melbourne, parks were laid out in a similar way to Peckham Rye Park and others nearby.

George Iggleden (Chichester), 1994

Children Yodelled

In the 1920s and '30s children would communicate with one another by emitting a special call similar to a yodel. They could be heard yodelling to one another on Goose Green and Peckham Rye as well as other places. Some could make a double or triple sound. I could not. I found it too difficult to do.

To my astonishment, my mother laughingly instructed me in the art of the perfect yodel. 'Oh yes, our generation communicated in the same way', she confided. Since the Second World War it has gradually vanished into the mists of time. Another tradition has disappeared with yesterday's children.

Grace Smith-Grogan, 2000

Watched Peacocks in Park

During the summer months relatives would sometimes book a tennis court in Peckham Rye Park. Occasionally I would be taken along with them to pick up and return their balls.

After the game we would go to the tea-rooms which were pleasantly situated beside the well-tended bowling green. There were round green metal tables with matching tip-up chairs arranged on the grass outside. To me, the most enjoyable feature was the tame peacocks who lived in the park. Three or four of them would stroll from table to table asking to be fed. If, as so often happened, they displayed their beautiful tails, this would be an added bonus!

I thought on these afternoons, how nice the family looked – the men with their cream flannel trousers, white open-necked shirts and navy blue blazers and the girls in white sleeveless dresses. The girls wore bandeaux when they were playing, in the fashion made popular at Wimbledon by the French tennis player Suzanne Lenglen.

If the weather was really fine and warm we would sometimes stay on in the park until the 'closing bells' were rung. The park-keepers in charge wore smart brown uniforms with matching trilby style hats. In the early evening, as the sun began to sink behind the trees, it was easy to appreciate William Blake's claim that, as a young child, he experienced his first vision on Peckham Rye. He described an oak tree, 'filled with angels, bright angelic wings bespangling every bough like stars!' For many years there was an old oak tree known as 'The Angel Oak' on Peckham Rye.

Strolling home from the park in the twilight, as dusk began to deepen, we would see the street lamplighter with his long pole moving between the posts, turning on the flickering yellow gas-lamps.

Joan Coxon, 2001

East Dulwich was Lovely

I was born in Bassano Street in 1936. I grew up and started my own family there in 1955, and then moved in 1961. The East Dulwich I remember was lovely with Goose Green and the Odeon Cinema; Dulwich Park

The Sexby Garden in Peckham Rye Park was an attractive feature on this postcard.

Donald Pooley stands in the Sexby Garden in Peckham Rye Park, c. 1941.

and Horniman Gardens were not far away. Dulwich Baths had two pools, a first and second class and public baths for people who didn't have bathrooms.

Joyce Woods (née Mason), 2000

Reading Books in the Library

Schoolchildren were encouraged to join Dulwich Library. Every Saturday I would walk along Barry Road. It seemed so long – nearly a mile I was told. In the library I browsed lazily through the children's section. I often sat in the library garden and quickly read a book before going back to exchange it for another one to take home.

Grace Smith-Grogan, 2000

Diced with Death

After an exciting day in Dulwich Park my friends and I would head for home and would dice with death on our roller skates, scooters and bikes coming down the Lordship Lane hill. We didn't stop at Townley Road and continued all the way to our homes.

Joyce Woods (née Mason), 2000

Firemen Remembered

Where the Telephone Exchange is today in Lordship Lane was a fire station. The fire engines had a gleaming brass bell and trimmings and the firemen wore shiny brass helmets. The path at the side is now called Fireman's Alley.

Brenda Pooley, 2001

Tennis was enjoyed in Peckham Rye Park.

Leaves on a path show that autumn has come to Peckham Rye Park.

Police officers, whose horses are stabled at East Dulwich Police Station, sometimes ride across Goose Green.

Dulwich Fire Station in Lordship Lane opened in 1893.

Dulwich Hospital was known as the Infirmary in the early twentieth century.

PC Percy Adkins and a
sergeant with his bicycle.

Recited Poetry on Hospital Radio

Some years ago, while recovering from an operation in Dulwich Hospital, I was asked if I would recite some of my poems for the hospital radio. While standing in a draughty corridor, with some people noisily rushing about, I recorded them. Surprisingly, the poetry came over very well.

There was a number of requests every day for more poems. Each time I was rewarded with a present, mostly Easter eggs – a large one the first day but decreasingly smaller ones as each day passed. Following that I was given several records of music by the Red Army Band.

One night I sat up late reciting to a large burly Scotsman who said the poetry helped to calm his nerves.

Grace Smith-Grogan, 2001

Presented with a Gold Watch

My father was PC 401 Percy Adkins who was based at East Dulwich Police Station for some years. We lived at No. 239 Lordship Lane. This was my home from 1929 until 1957 when I got married.

My dad served in the Great War at the age of seventeen. I have a gold watch given to my father and inscribed 'Presented to Ex-PC 401 P. Adkins by the East Dulwich Athletic Club in appreciation of his service while secretary 1926-1928.'

Barbara Rawle, 2001

CHAPTER 6

Recreation

WT. Cook (236) and L.W Recordon (124 not out) had a remarkable first wicket partnership for Honor Oak Cricket Club on Sunday 15 May 1927.

Watched Cricket

In the 1920s I watched Honor Oak Cricket Club play at the ground in Colyton Road where Homestall Road playing field is today. It was bigger in those days and the Club attracted good support from the spectators. There was wooden plank seating around much of the perimeter of the 1st/2nd XI playing area adjoining Colyton Road – and a gate was charged. In 1922 the receipts amounted to nearly £100 for the season.

A charity match against Guy's Hospital was played annually throughout the 1920s at Colyton Road in aid of various hospital charities. The last was played in 1931 after which the Club moved to Dulwich Common.

Maurice Alexander, 2000

Honor Oak Cricket Club's Second XI, 1922.

The Colyton Road ground, where Honor Oak Cricket Club played, 1908. The pavilion was on the Colyton Road boundary close to Homestall Road.

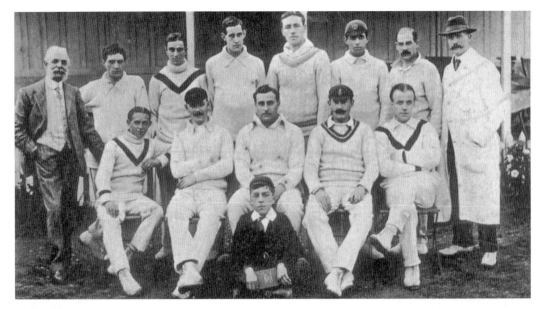

Honor Oak Cricket Club's team, 1913.

The team who played for Honor Oak Cricket Club, 1920.

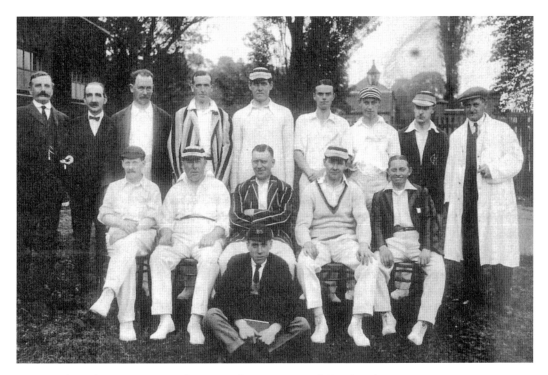

Honor Oak cricket team, 4 September 1929; the captain was G.A.J. Gawthorpe.

Possessed Few Toys

There were very few toys at home, so I often had to improvise or pretend. In imagination I could have had the richest toys that any child ever had and as many friends as were needed to enjoy them with me. So Sammy and Buzzy moved in to stay and were very economical of space since they were quite body-less! Their 'spirits' lived in the gap between the dresser and the wall and the door of the lower cupboard, in which the ginger spaniel, the humming top, the teddy bear, Joanie (the doll with the plaster face) and a stuffed doll were kept. The cupboard door made an excellent front door for their house. Just what an observer would have made of the game, I cannot tell.

Vera Conway, 1989

Enjoyed Goose Green Playground

My nan lived in Zenoria Street and when I visited her I often used to watch horses drinking from the trough where the nearby roundabout is today. From there I used to cut across Goose Green to the swing park which was the best as it had a maypole. I spent a lot of time on that and in the sandpit. There were also dual swings for two people to sit on at once plus a huge roundabout that seated dozens of kids. That was pyramid shaped but there was a smaller one called the bus, plus two rocking horses which each seated five or six. The slide and see-saw were popular.

Joyce Woods (née Mason), 2000

Tennis played in The Gardens

When I first came to live in The Gardens in the late 1920s most of the large houses were occupied by just one or two families. Mr and Mrs George Austin and family lived at No. 48. The park in the centre of The Gardens was used by the residents; it had two tennis courts which were very popular. These could be used by us children on Saturday mornings and at other times when not needed by the adults.

Elsie Blenkey, 2000

Accident at Wilson's fair

It was on VE day that I came to grief. Everyone was celebrating the end of the war in Europe. I was eight at the time. Some friends and I decided to celebrate by going to Wilson's fair near the Peckham Rye pond. I came a cropper on the switchback which suddenly stopped so I proceeded to get off. With one foot on the ground and one still on the platform, it started to spin out of control. My left leg got trapped between the moving platform and the stationary one.

The fairground manager didn't wait for an ambulance. He took me to Dulwich Hospital with my leg wrapped in a white towel which wasn't white on arrival at the hospital. That was not surprising as I had a compound fracture of the tibia and fibula. I was lucky not to lose the leg.

Joyce Woods (née Mason), 2000

Toys were Handmade

A lot of toys used to be handmade. My dad made me a scooter with a wooden upright and footboard. He used metal milk bottle tops to decorate the front. My granddad made me a dolls' house and all the furniture.

My most treasured articles were my stilts made by my dad. They were made from two upright pieces of wood with a tapered piece at the top to grip on and shaped pieces of wood attached a quarter of the way up to stand on. I often used mine to get my dad's *Evening News* from Mr Spring who had a newspaper stand outside the Lord Palmerston pub. I used to put the paper down my jumper and hobble back. It was great fun.

Joyce Woods (née Mason), 2000

Made Models

In the 1940s foundations were laid in Townley Road, near my new prefab home in Lordship Lane, to tether a big silver balloon. Out of the earth tumbled great lumps of yellow London clay – I was in my element. Nothing could stop me trekking to and fro as often as possible to collect this wonderful modelling material which no one else in the world appeared to have discovered. With sticky yellow fingers, my father and I made all kinds of models, from cups and saucers to animals, letting our imagination run riot. One day I made a group of natives, an idea inspired by the flea grass that grew by the edge of our pathway. The natives all received flea grass skirts and were taken to school to be shown off. The teachers were full of admiration. I was the star of the day and rewarded from the staff room bounty ... with a Swiss bun! It was delicious. From then onwards, Swiss buns were known as 'teachers buns' in our family!

Vera Conway, 1989

Bell Ringers Called

When I moved into Bawdale Road in the 1980s hand-bell ringers called in December instead of carol singers.

Sheila Hearsum, 2000

Goose Green

Enormous plane trees whose home is the
village green
Spreading leafy branches like huge
umbrellas
sheltering the meadow grass.
Generations of feet traverse the well worn
path
between the lofty trees.
From crinolines to denim jeans
Fashions change but not the scene
Dogs still roll and romp
Children picnic, bands play, fetes flourish
Green leaves turn to autumn gold
burnishing the seats beneath
Shady boughs compassionate, observe it all
Last year, this year, forever, until the
world's end.

Grace Smith-Grogan, August 2000

Photographed when Young

When I was coming along my parents bought a house in East Dulwich recommended by a member of a photographers' club to which my father belonged. How we children suffered under his hobby. We had to sit still for minutes, which seemed like hours, in those early days of photography. My brother, Will, must have resented this because my father enlarged one of him sitting on a stool in the garden with an angry scowl on his face! Then there was one of me, with a fixed look too scared to breathe even, so father told me to look away, I suppose to relieve the tension, but the result was an unnatural coy look!

Gwendoline Morris in her autobiography
Go East Young Woman (1996)

Swam in Dulwich Baths

Adys Road School was situated on the boundary of Peckham (SE15) and East Dulwich (SE22). I was a pupil there until 1928 having gone up from the infants at the age of seven. Reaching the age of twelve years entitled one to swimming on Tuesday afternoon.

Armed with a rolled-up towel and swimsuit (a full regulation navy blue type), the class assembled at 2 o'clock and in very orderly fashion went two by two, escorted by a teacher, across Goose Green, up the steps of the Dulwich Baths to the second-class bath. The allocation was two boys to each cubicle to get changed and into the water.

Somehow, most boys learnt how to swim and obtained their 40 yards certificate, even though the swimming season was just a few weeks in the summer and some twenty minutes in the water each week.

The season usually ended with a swimming gala in the first class pool on a Saturday evening. All boys could take part. Any non-swimmers had a wading event. My swimming prowess wasn't brilliant, so in the 40 yards event I clocked in last and was awarded a consolation prize of a propelling pencil!

Leonard R. Moncrieff (Canada), 2001

Happy Times with Hoops

I could go on and on about Christmas parties and summer outings with St John's church and what happy days they were with our hoops and skates. One wonders whether the children of today get as much pleasure from the simple things as we did.

Elsie Stukings, 1976

Edwardian Childhood Days in East Dulwich

I have lived in my house for eighty years so you can guess I have seen a few changes. I started school at St John's when I was three years old; Miss Huxley was the headmistress. She used to come and meet me and sometimes carry me when I didn't want to go. She was a lovely lady, liked by all. We paid 1d in the infants, 2d for the girls and 3d for the boys.

I can remember my father taking me to see fairy lights in Barry Road. My sister and I often went to Peckham Rye Park. The entrance then was facing the Friern Road School. We used to go and feed the ducks. There were some lovely peacocks there and we waited to see them show off their beautiful feathers. There used to be a lake on Peckham Rye where children sailed their boats. On Bank Holidays there used to be stalls round the Rye and donkey rides. There were no cars then. There were horse-buses, green and red. An old gentleman with a long white beard used to sit on a stool outside the East Dulwich Hotel and look after the cab horses, while the visitors went to have a drink. He was a Mr Lane and was the first baker in Crystal Palace Road. I can remember horse-trams running up that road. They had open sides; I was fascinated to watch the driver with his long whip. Dog Kennel Hill had seats for people to rest. The road was not wide and hawthorn hedges grew at the sides.

Elsie Sheppard in *Memories of the Good and Bad Old Days of Childhood* contributed by some East Dulwich people (St John's church, 1976)

Childhood Days in East Dulwich

In those days, children had to make their own pleasures; we could not sit and passively enjoy television, or even radio. Yet we managed to be happy, although deprived of pleasures which we could not possibly imagine. We chased one another across Peckham Rye; we followed the traditional season of children's games and we went, sometimes rather unwillingly, to school. Ah yes, school, where we were well disciplined and thoroughly taught. We did all the things, willy-nilly, which we are told today that children must never be subjected to. We learned by rote; we repeated our tables in unison; we knew all the parts of speech by the time we were eleven. What a different picture today, when an inspector was heard to complain that a school she was inspecting was too quiet. She wanted to hear noise, for 'Noise means work, noise means activity'. We dared not for our lives make any noise. The cane was freely used. I was in a favoured, if unenviable position, as form monitor, and had to keep a record of 'black marks' awarded for poor work. (Four 'black marks' and the luckless offender was caned.) Many were the sweets which I was offered to erase black marks from the record.

The pictures were a weekly delight. How we enjoyed the exciting serials, such as The Exploits of Elaine. There would be the heroine at the end of the episode, tied to the railway line for a week. How would she be saved, we wondered, until we watched goggle-eyed the next episode.

Pleasure cost little in those days. I remember a wonderful evening out for sixpence (2½ new pence).

A street party was held in Nutfield Road in 1935 to celebrate the Silver Jubilee of King George V. The shops are in North Cross Road.

The budget was as follows:

Tram to the Old Vic   1d
Seat in the gallery   3d
Tram home   1d
Chips from the fish shop   1d

'Bang goes sixpence'. But in those days men were bringing up families on £3 a week and sixpence a week pocket money was wealth untold.

Frederick Butcher in *Memories of the Good and Bad Old Days of Childhood* contributed by some East Dulwich people (St John's church, 1976)

No Money to Listen to Wireless

Where Sainsbury's car park is today was a rugby sports ground. In the 1920s a summer fair was held there. The main attraction was in a marquee – the new wonder – wireless. I remember gazing at all the people inside with headphones clamped to their ears. Unfortunately, I hadn't the 6d needed to join them.

Joseph Hack, 2001

Attended Band of Hope

One evening each week we would go to the Band of Hope which was held in the hall which is now the United Reformed church. We would have a sing-song and then be shown a film all about the demon drink! On our way out they would try and get us to sign the pledge and as we were scared by that film I think we would have signed anything.

Elsie Stukings, 1976

No Paper Costumes Allowed in Dulwich Baths

A fancy dress ball for children used to be held every year in Dulwich Baths. They could go in any costume provided that it was not made from paper or cotton wool in case there was a fire.

Grace Smith-Grogan, 2000

Watched Dulwich Hamlet Play

On Saturday afternoons I often accompanied my father to a Dulwich Hamlet football match. We would sit in the stand and I would enjoy watching all the flat caps moving left, right, left, right, as their owners watched the game intently. I listened to the comments like 'Foul, foul' and 'Where's your glasses ref?' Crowds were polite in those days; there were no hooligans. The players would shake hands when a goal was scored. There was no hugging or kissing. It was a gentlemen's game.

Grace Smith-Grogan, 2000

Mixed Bathing Introduced

I remember when mixed bathing was introduced at Dulwich Baths. To make things decent, canvas screens were erected along the sides so boys could not gaze at girls' legs beneath the 'horse box' doors. Boys wore revealing cotton swimsuits so we were given stiff canvas briefs to make us decent.

Joseph Hack, 2001

Crowned May Queen

The 7th East Dulwich Brownie Pack bestowed upon me the honorary title of 'Brown Owl's Husband Len'. My primary involvement with them was the annual May Queen Display. This was celebrated during early May and spanned the period around 1950-1960.

Around mid-January the Brownies would select who would be crowned for that year. The Brown Owl (and many helpers) would design a programme consisting of singing, games, dances, playlets and so forth. From then onwards there were the costumes to be made and fitted while rehearsals were being staged piece by piece each week. These were performed in the Methodist Church Hall in Upland Road, when the church with the spire was in Barry Road. I was asked to be a

Adults as well as children dressed up in 1935 during the street party in Nutfield Road.

witness, so to speak, just offering helpful hints when approached by Brown Owl, who was the producer.

Pre-show preparation required designing and duplicating the programmes, a task assigned to myself. The fancy costumes and other stage props were made by willing mothers and fathers at no expense to the Brownie pack.

The morning of the great day began by transforming the Church Hall into a 'Throne Room' and auditorium. Grandpa's favourite armchair was converted into an elegant throne with masses of coloured drapes and flowers. Here would sit the chosen May Queen with her attendants on each side. These were usually the younger sisters of the Brownies. A final full dress rehearsal was performed in readiness for the evening show. This was always a full house.

An item in the 1957 show was the 'Pony Trot'.

Leonard Moncrieff, 2001

Went to the Bug Hutch

In Grove Vale was a small cinema known to us as the Bug Hutch but officially called the Pavilion. We sat sideways in the gallery. I was a frequent customer as it was only a few minutes' walk from my home in Muschamp Road.

Joseph Hack, 2001

Became Good Templars

When I was fifteen and my sister was twenty-two we joined the International Order of Good Templars. Our parents had met through the Order years before. There was a Lodge in every district and they all had names – James Eaton in Nunhead, Peckham Five and Dulwich Victorious which was ours.

We met in the old Liberal Association rooms in Lordship Lane. To join, one had to go through an initiation ceremony. The words expressed were very old-fashioned and were

Children dressed up for the Nutfield Road street party.

A charity football match was played at Dulwich Hamlet Football Ground on 17 September 1978. Robert Powell and Dennis Waterman were among the celebrities who played.

read by a dear old gentleman reading from the service book. My sister and I suffered from suppressed laughter. I must say though it was a beautiful and moving service.

We were then ushered into a circle of people with joined hands singing 'Welcome, welcome to our order'. It is a wonderful movement in which to belong. Members are happy, friendly, cheerful people with a great sense of humour. We enjoyed social evenings, musical evenings and quizzes. We had a sports club, amateur dramatics, ballroom dances and a concert party named Ruby Revellers.

There were a lot of talented people from all backgrounds and age groups. Some Members of Parliament have attributed their gift of oratory in the House of Commons to their speech-making within the Good Templar Order.

A member could attend any Lodge anywhere and be instantly made welcome. A quarterly guide would list programmes. One could never be lonely. Our Lodge met once a week with a membership of 100 people. The main condition of membership was a promise not to drink alcohol. I have entertained a great many people including teenagers who found they could enjoy themselves without alcohol. People today who haven't experienced the pleasures of an alcohol-free lifestyle are missing a lot.

Grace Smith-Grogan, 2000

Played Different Games

We didn't buy many toys; even Christmas tended to be books or new clothes. My father made the toys that were among our favourites, such as the huge dolls' house and all the furniture to go inside it and the push-along horse that helped my little sister to learn to walk. One never knew what delights would emanate from my grandfather's workshop. He loved metal work and once he made a set of tiny cups and saucers with wire handles. These were, of course, in the days before plastic and I longed for things that quite simply hadn't been invented yet, such as small dolls to fit inside our dolls' house, ones with arms and legs that could

Dulwich Hamlet Football Ground, opened in 1931, was demolished to make way for a new ground that opened in 1992.

be moved rather than the chalk ones we had with their limbs stuck to their sides. Dad showed us how to make bows and arrows. What fun we had with those, never using them irresponsibly as some children might today.

Grandfather had us on the shove ha'penny board from a very early age. He had made the board from a piece of oak and we polished it with French chalk till it shone. We were good players and sometimes we won.

Someone gave dad a bagatelle board and the many hours we spent playing that game certainly had an effect on our mathematics. Five stones occupied us for hours; they could be bought very cheaply, or we could use ordinary stones and play different kinds of games with them,

Gran played cards with us for hours, playing snap, donkey, old maid, sevens or beat your neighbour. When we tired of those games on wet afternoons, we would use the cards to build houses until they all fell flat. We were rarely bored.

Vera Conway, 2001

Simple Games Enjoyed

One day Pat Grimsey had a birthday party in her grandma's house and we were all invited. It was to be a 'dressing up' party and we were scheduled to make a play about Sleeping Beauty. I cannot remember the success of the play but we certainly all enjoyed dressing up. How we loved to get hold of some 'grown-ups' shoes and to clonk around in them or put a net curtain over our heads and pretend to be 'brides'!

I am sure that we were very well behaved as we played so happily and contentedly in our street. Expected standards of behaviour were much higher than they are today and householders would have been fearfully

angry if we had seriously offended them, but we had one 'naughty game' which we enjoyed very much. It was called 'Knock Down Ginger'. We would simply knock on someone's door, then run and hide and watch as our victim came to open the door and 'reacted' very mildly, as a rule. Oh the excitement of knocking and running to hide! The giggles, the bated breath, the stillness and the silence ... and the shrieks when our more cunning prey hid behind the door awaiting our second knock and caught us red-handed!

So many games come to mind. Skipping rope was easily obtained as most windows were the sash cord type and rope was sold for their repair. If we could get hold of a long piece that would stretch across the road from pavement to pavement, the possibilities of our games could be extended. We could play 'higher and higher', with the 'enders' raising the rope a little more each time we 'jumpers' came round for our next turn. If any part of us came into contact with the rope as we jumped over, we were 'out' and had to relieve an ender. Sometimes, calling 'salt, mustard, vinegar, pepper' we ran into the rope as the person in front of us ran out of it. Jumping 'over the moon', or running 'under the stars' could be quite difficult if the rope was turned swiftly, but we were clever! How we loved to chant, 'I'll tell Ma of Mary Ann, walking down the street with a nice young man. High heeled shoes and a feather in her hat. I'll tell Ma, the saucy old cat! I'll tell Ma when I get home, the boys won't leave the girls alone. They pull my hair and break my comb, I'll tell Ma when I get home.' My grandmother knew some of these rhymes too, from her own childhood days. Though in her late fifties she was not averse to jumping in the rope with us, much to the amusement of all the children!

We sang 'One, two, three, Alairee, my ball's on the area, go and fetch it Mary, one,

The 7th East Dulwich Brownie Pack performed the *Pony Trot* at Barry Road Methodist church in 1957.

two, three Alairee'. When this chant ended, we had to run out of the rope while it was still turning.

'Snakes and ladders' kept us hopping! Snakes were made by twitching the rope sideways on the road and ladders by moving the rope up and down. We all had to jump over without getting 'bitten'. 'All in together girls' had a row of us laughing and jostling in the rope together as it turned – and woe betide anyone who jumped at the wrong moment! The difficulty of that game was increased as we joined the line and jumped in one at a time.

The summer evenings seemed endless; summer holidays were long and full of wonderful sunshine. If our street was not the best place to play in, and some people even in those days deplored children playing in the street because they had heard about 'evil communications corrupting good manners', then I look back thankfully, remembering that in our play we acted out those happier scenes which lifted us above the environmental deficits and the sorrows of our age.

The girls I played with were no more 'evil' than I was and I can think of no evil thing that I learnt from them nor any harm that ever came to me because I enjoyed their company. They were all lovely children who could, generally speaking, be trusted to behave themselves away from the eagle eyes of their parents. I often wonder where they all are now. We spent hours playing 'mothers and fathers', putting dolls to bed, pouring out cups of pretend tea, and serving up 'meals' on plates using stones, leaves or seeds to resemble food.

Our houses were the little front gardens of the home in our street and the window sills were shelves, kitchens, tables, beds or whatever our vivid imaginations required of them. We were all secure in the knowledge that our parents were at home just a little way away should we need them.

A piece of chalk was a real treasure and enabled us to draw a hopscotch on the pavement. Players had to throw a stone into the square numbered 1 and hop into the square, retrieve the stone without putting another foot down, then hop back to the starting line. The stone then had to be thrown into square 2 and so on. Anything that would write on the pavement could be used to draw a hopscotch, even a piece of brick or plaster.

Vera Conway, 2001

Played in Road

The children of Chesterfield Grove played in the road quite safely spending many happy hours on their scooters and bikes or playing hopscotch, conkers, spinning tops and skipping. We used to have an old washing line stretched across the road. It was heavy to turn but we all joined in skipping games like 'All in together this frosty weather'.

We loved to play hide and seek behind the huge trunks of the chestnut and plane trees which lined the road. We also hid behind people's hedges as every house had a neatly cut privet hedge. There was a man who lived along the road who used to take a chair out to the middle of the road and climb on it so that he could make sure he had cut his hedge quite straight! Sadly the ornate iron railings and gates which fronted each house were removed for the war effort.

Gill Harding, 2001

The East Dulwich Estate at Dog Kennel Hill overlooked King's College Sports Ground where cricket was enjoyed until half the grass was covered with tarmac for a road and Sainsbury's car park.

Games were Exciting

We often played with balls and we were clever with them. 'Two balls' needed a nice, smooth, brick wall and we knew where they all were and had our favourites. Besides juggling the two (or even three) balls there were other skilful moves in this game such as passing the ball underneath one leg while the other ball was on the way down from the wall. Sometimes a ball was bounced regularly as a part of the routine, 'dropped' we would say.

Football was seldom played in the street. It was permitted in the school playground, but breaking windows, even accidentally, was a serious offence as repairs were costly. Walls were useful for other games too; we used them in our acrobatic activities particularly for 'handstands' for which we would tuck our skirts into our navy blue drawers to render our upside down position more respectable!

'Peep behind the curtain' was a game that was much enjoyed; a leader, chosen by 'dipping', 'One potato, two potato, three potato four, five potato, six potato, seven potato more'. The potatoes were our fists which we held out in front of us. On the word 'more' the fist that was touched had to be put behind the back. Fists were eliminated until one remained and the owner was 'he'. Sometimes we sang 'Round and round the butter dish, one, two, three, please little maid, will you be "he"? Then we shall see. O.U.T. spells OUT!' 'He' stood with his or her back to the other players as they crept forward. Suddenly, 'he' would turn to look at them and anyone who was seen moving was 'out'. The game continued until one player could touch the leader and become leader for the next game.

In another game, the leader would call out directions to the players. 'Two watering cans' meant that we all had to spit forward and jump to where our spittle landed. 'Two twisters' meant that we had to spin round twice and move forward in the spin. 'Four pigeon steps' were made by putting heel to toe and those with the biggest feet benefited. There were 'giant steps', hops or 'crabs' (walking sideways) all with the aim of touching the leader before anyone else got there.

'Please Mr Frog may we cross your water?' 'Yes, if you are wearing ...' blue, green, pink, red and so on. The others had to try to get across without being caught. The road was the 'water' and we lined up along the kerb. If we had a favourite game, it must have been 'Hide and Seek'. We would set a boundary, 'No one's to go out of the street', then the chosen 'seeker' would cover his or her eyes, count to ten and call, 'Coming'.

Oh, the excitement, the joy, the laughter, the thrill! What could compare with our involvement? So often we went home to bed hot, dirty, happy and so contented.

Vera Conway, 2001

Went Scrumping

We used to go to the local parks and Horniman's Museum. At the back of Horniman's were open fields where we used to pick blackberries and my three brothers used to go scrumping. As I was the only girl I was the lookout and we would fill our pockets with crab apples and eat them all. In the middle of the night we all had tummy ache and mother would think it was something she had given us. We dare not say a word, so we all had castor oil in the morning – serve us right!

Elsie Stukings, 1976

The Cherry Tree pub was demolished to make way for what today is The Vale.

Went 'Fishing'

Discipline was important and my father kept a cane. It hung in the wardrobe amongst the clothing. My knowledge of its presence there meant that dad hardly ever had to use it, as fear of 'getting the cane' kept us within bounds. However, I was not a good little girl and sometimes my independence clashed with my parents' wishes. Staying in the street was a rule to be generally observed, but one evening adventure got the better of me, and I went fishing. The tank in which the fishes were supposed to reside was situated in Melbourne Grove, almost opposite the end of Blackwater Street and built on a bomb site. It was supposed to be a reservoir for emergency supplies of water, but few of these tanks ever contained more than a little rainwater that fell into them. I was, however, convinced that there was something worth catching in the tank and that I had the wherewithal to extract the creature, namely, the pin in my plaid skirt. So involved were we without rods and lines that we paid no attention to the passing of time or the setting sun, so it was with some terror that I observed my father's face as he came striding down Blackwater Street to find me!

Vera Conway, 2001

Played in Streets

We played in the streets – skipping and 'higher and higher' with the rope stretched across the street – no cars in sight; we might have to lower our rope for an occasional push bike – hopscotch, bowling hoops, riding scooters and roller skates. In our back gardens we played 'mothers and fathers', 'doctors and nurses' and 'schools'.

Fairs on Peckham Rye and King's College sports ground on Dog Kennel Hill; saluting the flag on Empire Day followed by a half-day's holiday; saving our pennies in a Firework club; being sent with a shilling to get dad 20 Players and being allowed to spend the halfpenny change on Tiger nuts, aniseed balls or a liquorice strip, whichever delicacy took our fancy at the time; the smell of Christmas puddings boiling, and clean curtains at the kitchen window which heralded the coming Christmas – the memories are endless and they added up to a happy childhood for me.

Hilda Kors, 1976

Keen Cinema Goer

I vaguely remember seeing the Odeon Cinema being built; it opened in 1938. We lived at No. 40 Oakhurst Grove at that time. Some time later my mother took me there to see Will Hay in *Oh Mr Porter*. I also went with my mates on Saturday mornings; it was usually very noisy.

There was always a serial to make us come back – usually a Western one. One film that sticks in my mind was *Flash Gordon's Trip to Mars* which was a pre-war science fiction film. Around this period I also saw *It's in the Air* with George Formby, Shirley Temple in *Rebecca of Sunnybrook Farm* and *Rose Marie* and *Bitter Sweet* with Jeanette MacDonald and Nelson Eddy.

We moved to Rye Hill Estate, Peckham Rye East, so going to the cinema in East Dulwich meant riding on a tram which was an extra thrill.

The outbreak of war spoilt all this. I was evacuated to Dorking and then to Yorkshire until the war had ended. I returned to London an ardent fan and soon became a regular cinema-goer – often three or four times a week. One thing I liked about the Odeon was the car park. Though we didn't have a car, my brother and I used to sweep into the car park on our bikes, lock them up, remove our cycle clips and stroll nonchalantly into the cinema. There at the front of house would be the manager, Mr Slatter, all resplendent in his full dress suit. The foyer was spacious and the cinema was

oddly wider than its length. For a small cinema it had an enormous screen. If you sat in the circle you felt you were actually in the screen.

Those were happy days. My father always said that I should have had a bed in the Odeon which we fondly called Slatters House.

Winifred MacKenzie, 2000

Joke Shop was Popular

The 'joke shop' in Grove Vale held a fascination for children. The famous itching powder and sneezing powder were great fun. The realistic tin daggers, whose blade pushed back into the handle when thrust into the so-called victim, were quite safe.

Masks, moustaches, beards, wigs and conjuring tricks were good but the most popular were the little strips of pink 'caps'. When placed inside a toy gun they made an ear-splitting noise after the trigger was pulled. Some boys and girls placed them on the paving stones and then stamped on them one by one. The explosions startled their friends. An acrid smell of gunpowder followed.

Grace Smith-Grogan, 2001

Stage Set up in Street

At the very end of the war after VJ night there were great celebrations. I can remember the Italian man who had a home-made ice cream shop opposite St John's School wheeling his cart outside the school gates and giving each child a free ice cream cornet – it was delicious! Most streets had parties for the children in the daytime but on many Saturday evenings after the war ended there were much grander ones for the adults.

The word would go round where a stage was being set up in a particular street and anyone with some entertaining talent would take part. There were many good pianists, singers and small dance bands. I used to go along with my sisters and a grand time was had by all.

Gill Harding, 2001

Crystal Palace Burnt

I was born on 22 May 1931 in Camberwell but four years later we moved to No. 14 Goldwell House, Quorn Road.

While my parents were in the Cherry Tree pub, we kids ran around the estate playing chase. On 30 November 1936 kids ran around shouting, 'Fire! fire!'. When we asked where, they said, 'On top of Doggy' (Doggy was short for Dog Kennel Hill). So we rushed there. We stood with our mouths wide open. The sky was lit up like a thousand searchlights as we watched Crystal Palace burning.

H.T. Benton, 2001

Wireless Entertainment

My brother was born in Dulwich Hospital in 1932. I remember standing in the crowd near the hospital during carnival time. In the procession were men with huge and hideous heads. I was terrified of them.

Like everyone else, our usual entertainment apart from the wireless was the pictures. My first film was *The Vagabond King*.

On 5 November, having waved our sparklers around in the backyard, we walked up to the top of Dog Kennel Hill from where we could see the fireworks at Crystal Palace. I can just remember going to this huge glass place and seeing exhibits from the Empire. We stood in our back garden in Nunhead in 1936 and watched the distant glow as the wireless told us that Crystal Palace was on fire. The gardens were one of our favourite visits but I was terrified of the dinosaurs.

Christine Brock, 2001

Tea after Cup Final

In my possession is a letter sent from No. 26 Friern Road. The postmark on the envelope is AP 17 01 (17 April 1901) and the one penny stamp has the head of Victoria on it. The letter was sent by Gertie Flower (née Windley) to her sister Miss Florrie Windley in Chesterfield, Derbyshire. Florrie was my granny.

The letter suggests that Florrie's sweetheart, Albert, and his friend come to her home for tea after visiting 'the Palace' – Crystal Palace – for 'the Final on Saturday'. She was referring to the Cup Final played on 20 April 1901 when Tottenham Hotspur drew 2-2 with Sheffield United in front of a crowd of 114,815.

Kathleen Harper (Devon), 2001

CHAPTER 7

Places of Worship

Sheep grazed on Goose Green close to St John the Evangelist church, *c.* 1865.

St John's during the First World War

I seem to have spent my life around St John's. Mr Read was the vicar at that time and at his insistence I joined the Catechism which was then conducted by Father Stacey, a rather swarthy, austere gentleman. I duly presented myself to him when I was asked my name, address and how old I was. Upon my telling him I was twelve, he looked askance and said I was a big person for twelve, as indeed I was. He then asked me whether I had been

In 1929 St John the Evangelist church had thriving organizations called the Senior Catechism

St John the Evangelist church at Goose Green was consecrated in 1865.

baptised and I said I had. He then said, 'Of course you have not been confirmed'. I was so staggered by the fact that he thought I was a big person for my age and took it for granted I had not been confirmed, that I immediately answered, 'Yes, indeed, I was confirmed when I was eleven'.

As a family we attended St John's for the first time at the Three Hours Service on Good Friday 1918 and I remember mother being really scared of the crowds that queued outside the church for the various services.

How well I remember the fancy dress parties with our good friend and wonderful Verger Jimmy Holliday well to the fore. I was dressed as Good Luck for my first fancy dress party and still, very proudly, have the photograph to remind me of that event.

Most of the houses around Adys Road were of the small villa type with neatly trimmed hedges and the large houses in East Dulwich Road, Oakhurst Grove and The Gardens were privately owned mostly having their servants.

Elsie Moody in *Memories of the Good and Bad Old Days of Childhood*, contributed by some East Dulwich people (St John's church, 1976)

and the Junior Catechism. This photograph was taken in the playground of Adys Road School.

Apologised for Lateness

The Revd S.F. Hawkes was a forceful preacher. I have never forgotten one of his injunctions from the pulpit, 'If you come in late, don't march up to the front but sneak into a back pew and apologise to God'.

Among his many activities, Father Hawkes was responsible for the erection of our war memorial, the Calvary in our church garden, which was later consecrated as the burial ground for the ashes of St John's people. He also installed a disused army hut in the old vicarage garden at the corner of Crystal Palace Road to serve as a hall.

Nora Cullingford in *My Decade of Vicars of St John's*, East Dulwich (1977)

Garden backs on to St John's Church

My house backs on to St John the Evangelist church; it looms up the other side of the dividing stone garden wall. I have lovely memories of sitting in my garden listening to the organist practising, silhouetted against the window. I can picture lights streaming though a stained glass window pane on a murky, foggy evening.

At the end of the church there was a beautiful view across Goose Green. I saw weddings with brides and grooms photographed at the west door. Wedding guests chatted to us through the chain link fence we erected to top the low stone church wall.

I remember Violet Tucker, their dedicated lady gardener, sitting on that wall chatting to us about the delights of gardening and swapping ideas. Year after year she was always there. After she departed this earthly life in 2000 her ashes were interred in the lovely Calvary garden she had helped to maintain.

The Goose Green Community Centre has changed the surroundings and blocked us all in. However, I can still see the top of the tall London plane trees and visualise in my mind's eye people walking their dogs, as well as summer fairs and carnivals.

Opposite, in East Dulwich Road, an old house stood next to Dulwich Baths. A friend of mine once lived there during the Second World War and afterwards. As young married women without telephones,

The Duchess of Marlborough visited Dulwich Baths on 25 November 1908 to open Ye Olde Dulwyche Fayre which was held for four days to raise funds for St John's School and Epiphany Mission church belonging to St John the Evangelist church. Stalls represented various periods of English history including 'Atte ye signe of Ye Whyte Rose' (Charles II). The picture shows scouts only a year after the Scout Association was formed.

books or played quietly with our toys. We would go to church, very often to the 11 o'clock service and we would all be dressed in our Sunday best. I thought I looked very chic – black woollen stockings, buttoned boots, grey coat and silver-grey muff and fur, a black velour hat with bright red cherries round the brim and two pigtails tied with red ribbon. We children always used to make for the gallery which was over the present Lady Chapel. We used to look down at the congregation and see the pews with the family names on them. We thought they were very rich, as the ladies wore fur coats and the men wore cravats and carried silver-topped canes in their hands. The brass Eagle glinted on the lectern and the preacher used to climb into the pulpit to preach fire and brimstone and that we were all sinners. Sometimes I used to think he would fall out of the pulpit with his actions. I used to pray to God to make me a good girl, ignoring the boy behind me who was pulling my pigtails. But my good intentions soon went by the board when we got out of church and I found the boy had pulled the cherries off my hat at the back; so I chased him and called him all the names imaginable. Well, I was punished for that as we were not supposed to run on a Sunday, let alone call names. The favourite punishment was to be sent to bed early. I didn't mind that, as I always put a book under my mattress; and as I am very fond of reading, it was no punishment.

Elsie Stukings, 1976

we would signal to one another by placing a large white card in an upstairs window which meant 'Come over, I have something interesting to reveal'.

This method of communication was possible only during autumn and winter when the trees had shed their leaves; we could see through the gap. Happy days!

Grace Smith-Grogan, 2000

Attended St John's

Sunday was children's service at the Epiphany Hall in the morning and Sunday School classes in the afternoon where we learnt the Catechism. In the evening we read religious

Church was Active

For many years I was a choirboy and server at St John the Evangelist church. In the 1920s and '30s the church ran Sunday Schools in local schools – Grove Vale, Adys Road and Bellenden Road.

At Christmas, the Dulwich Baths were hired for a fayre. The small bath was turned into a children's fayre with coconut shies and games. Also at Christmas there was a fancy dress ball. We older guys would dress up at the Vicarage, on the corner of Crystal Palace Road.

In the summer a train was hired to take us from East Dulwich Station for a day out at Bognor.

The Scouts and Guides had summer camps. About 150 young 'civilians' went camping in Devon, Dorset and Oxfordshire. An advance party, including myself, erected the tents and marquee.

Joseph Hack, 2001

Cavalry Garden, St John's Church

Jesus looks down from His Cross
to the quiet garden below
Flowers curtsy at His feet
as soft the breezes blow.

Fine lawn of green surround Him
Flowering bushes sway
as butterflies and insects
wing their busy way.

A blackbird on a bough
sings his tuneful 'Evensong'
when twilight drops her veil
on the crowned Head of all.

Such beauty in this garden
an oasis 'mid life's storms
The loving hands of the gardener
whose labour creates and warms.

Grace Smith-Grogan, August 2000

Hall was a Boon

The Epiphany Hall in Bassano Street belonged to St John's church and was a great boon to everybody. We had magic lantern shows there and the Brownies, Guides and Scouts had their meetings there.

My sister was christened in the Epiphany Hall and two of my aunts were married there. It was also used for games and sports. The church part was downstairs and the social events were held upstairs.

Joyce Woods (née Mason), 2000

Became an Altar Boy

My first school was St John's in North Cross Road. Pupils were encouraged to attend church on Sunday. Services were held in the Epiphany Hall in Bassano Street.

As I regularly attended a club meeting which took place in the hall above where the services were held, I was asked to become an altar boy. This meant that I carried the incense boat.

I remember taking part in a procession from St John's church on Goose Green to the Epiphany Hall via Adys Road, East Dulwich Road, Lordship Lane and Bassano Street. This happened before the church was repaired after being badly damaged by bombing.

Peter Morris, 2001

Sang with Collection

At the age of four I was taken to the beginner's department of Emmanuel church in Barry Road where my mother's family had attended and where my parents were married. I enjoyed this very much.

In 1946 Frank Soames married Nellie Brown in the Epiphany Hall, Bassano Street. The hall was used for services until the bombed St John the Evangelist Church was reopened in 1951.

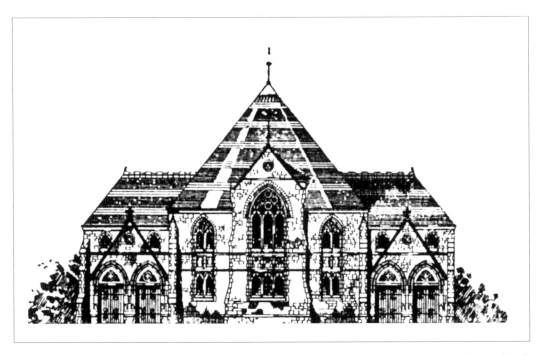

Emmanuel Congregational Sunday School Hall which was built in 1898 and converted into Christ Church in 1988.

An iron chapel, opened in 1877, was used before Emmanuel Congregational church was built in Barry Road. It was demolished in 1898 when the present Christ Church was built on the site.

One thing I remember when promoted to the Primary Department is that we marched around with our collection singing 'Hear the pennies dropping'. In fine weather we marched out of the door, round the passage outside and back in the other.

Brenda Pooley, 2001

Attended Seances

One dark night, my girlfriend Margaret and I entered the front precincts of Barry Road Methodist church and proceeded to the rear of the church where there was a flight of rickety wooden stairs leading to a wooden door. On knocking on the door, it was opened with a suitable creaking and squeaking musical accompaniment to reveal a stooped lady of advancing years.

We were invited in to join a number of people already seated on perhaps ten rows of bench seats. The next thing I remember was that we sang a hymn after which the lady became distinctly vacant while standing on a little stage. She asked if there was anyone who knew ... Tom, Dick or Harry, and of course there was!

After about ten minutes of this the 'medium' moved around to various people to pass on messages 'from beyond'. Strangely, she had none for me, no doubt because I had decided that if she had any telepathic abilities she was going to be out of luck with me. I believe there was a collection at the end.

Out of experimental curiosity (due to a scientific background) I returned to a second session at the seance. This time, I made no attempt to blank out any thoughts. When she paused at me, I was told that my father had died (which he had, fifteen years before),

Cecil Pooley and Winifred Chinneck were married at Emmanuel Congregational Church on 15 June 1929.

Emmanuel Congregational church opened in 1891.

my writing was too small, and that I should be careful with noisy machinery.

Four years later I had a bad motor-cycle accident in Germany and broke a couple of ribs. The 'medium' made no mention of any future with Margaret, who eventually married John Fitchet.

The only conclusion that I can draw from the above encounters is that there was possibly a slight telepathic ability (suitably embroidered) which enhanced the performance of the seance. As for the motor-cycle accident, most young men had a motor-cycle and accidents on wet tar surfaces riddled with wet tram-lines were a feature of everyday life.

Stanley Kettel, 2000

Taught in Sunday School

On Sundays I went to morning church. I was a Sunday school teacher at Emmanuel Congregational church, Barry Road, and took a class in the afternoon. By this time I wanted to join the youth club which meant I had to join the Emmanuel church and give up the Girls' Brigade. It was lovely and I enjoyed going. We had coca cola, lemonade and crisps. We learned how to do square dancing.

Sheila Davidson, 2001

Went to the Epiphany Hall

While we were in the top class at St John's School we had a student teacher for a while. We very soon took to the tall young man with dark hair. Mr Jordan was very interested in astronomy and passed on some of his knowledge about the universe to us. How we romantic little girls, no doubt relating to some story or other in the *Girls' Crystal*, hoped that Miss Mingay and Mr Jordan would marry and live happily ever after! We certainly made up all kinds of stories for them! Stories were our entertainment; we relied heavily on the BBC Children's Hour and loved the tales that were read and acted over the air. Miss Mingay read to us each day, sometimes serialising a book and best of all I remember her reading *Little Women* by Louisa M. Alcott. We could hardly wait for the next day and the next instalment.

The fact that we were a church school, that we belonged to St John's church, was definitely not forgotten. In the top class we were prepared for confirmation, though I do not remember any of my peer group actually taking the step. A lady came every week to drill us in the Creed and the Catechism. We were required, on occasions, to recite the results of her labours to Father Bishop, or later, to Father MacKenzie who succeeded him though I do not remember when the change came.

At some time we attended the Epiphany Hall on consecutive Wednesday mornings to take part in a children's service. The service was written in narrow green books and we learned the order of praying, singing and listening as we followed the directions. During the prayers it was the custom to swing censers, and some of the boys were dressed in white, chosen for the task. Yes, I do remember David Morris had to do it once! At this point in the proceedings it was normal for several children to faint! There seemed to be no medical reason for this falling sickness, unless some kind of mass hysteria spread through the congregation, but those who succumbed were hastily removed to the fresh air of Bassano Street! The church at Goose Green had been severely damaged during the war, so we were never taken there. The Epiphany Hall was our church and I remember it being pleasantly warm and welcoming as a building. For a little while before we moved, I attended Girl Guide meetings in the hall above the church and I think it was Miss Foster who took an active part in the company. We saved our pennies for the electric light and ringing in our ears was the promise of a brand new school, one day. St John's was always too small for comfort though we were less troubled by that than the teachers were! It is good to remember the place with affection and to have such good, conscientious, kind people etched forever upon one's mind. Mrs Wilson, the headmistress ... I would hardly be surprised to see her standing in the playground next time I pass by! She was a strict lady, stout and slightly bewhiskered and always dressed in a green suit. Mrs Billis was the deputy head ... I was never in her class and knew little about her, but who can forget her fascinating twitch which stretched and relaxed her mouth. Miss Blofield said to my mother, 'That girl has piano fingers.' It was a pity that I did not have a piano to go with them!

I could go on! Many small memories crowd in until it is the gaps in my memory that puzzle me most. If time has blurred the accuracy of any detail, I hope there will be someone to put me right!

Vera Conway, 1989

Joined Choir

We were not a church-going family, but I recall my aunt taking me to a Toy Service at

Scaffolding surrounded the spire of Barry Road Methodist church.

Scotland hall in Worlingham Road.

After the church parade in mid-winter we walked home but made a detour to the lido on Peckham Rye where we climbed over the wall and had a quick private dip in the nude.

Stanley Kettel, 2000

Bought a Haggis

Years ago I went to the Christmas Market at St James's Church of Scotland in East Dulwich Road and bought a haggis. I took it home and sliced it daintily then served it with vegetables. Disappointingly, we found it very tough and tasteless – and the texture was coarse. I found out later that it should have been well cooked. Our bottle of magnesia was very depleted that weekend!

Grace Smith-Grogan, 2000

St Peter's in Lordship Lane. My parents had been married in St Clement's in Friern Road; I was christened there.

In 1946, realising the gap in my life, I went to Barry Road Methodist church where I joined the choir and was soon involved in other activities. Since 1966 I have been a Methodist Local Preacher and enjoy taking part in activities at Christ Church in Barry Road.

Christine Brock, 2001

Joined Sea Cadets

I was born in Grenard Road, Peckham, in 1925 and in 1940 joined the Dulwich Sea Cadets. I received very valuable training as a precursor to joining the Royal Navy two years later. The Sea Cadets were run by Commander Cole in St James's church of

Enjoyed Girls' Life Brigade

I joined the Girls' Life Brigade which I adored. It was held in the hall of the Baptist Church in Lordship Lane on the corner of Goodrich Road. It was much like Brownies and Guides. We worked on projects such as learning about knots. If we passed the test we got a badge to sew on the sleeve of our uniforms. These were navy blue serge dresses with long sleeves, a high neck with a collar and some red piping around the collar. I think we wore a beret. We also learned to dance, to skip, to do gymnastics and all sorts of things. Each year we put on a display in which we showed off these new skills.

I fondly remember a synchronised skipping show. We all wore little white dresses. Our parents came to watch.

We went to church parades when we all marched from a given point down the road to the church in a parade preceded by our banner carrier. We then had to sit through an interminable sermon in the church.

Occasionally, we would meet up with other groups in another place, such as Norwood, and there would be a mass parade. Once a year there would be a marvellous display in the Albert Hall. It was wonderful if we were chosen to take part and I well remember the synchronised skipping show there with hundreds of girls performing. I loved this. We took a packed lunch and went up to London in a coach. It was all so exciting running around all those little rabbit warrens of dressing rooms in the Albert Hall, having lunch across the road and experiencing the excitement and pride of being in the display.

As children we went to the Odeon in Grove Vale to Saturday morning pictures for a shilling.

Sheila Davidson, 2001

Sisters Died

The deaths of my sisters, each at the age of seven, completely changed our lives. My elder sister Kathleen died in 1912, on the same night as the Titanic sank. I was only a year old. My younger sister Sylvia died in 1920, when I was nine years old. At first my parents were angry with God but with the wise and sympathetic solace given by our Scottish family doctor Dr James Ebenezer Boon and the spiritual succour of the church, they were able to understand and come to terms with the deaths and accept Him and His goodness. Even more than before, the Church came to play a major part in all our lives. We all went to church regularly but due to friends and other influences, we eventually came to belong to different churches. Though my parents had originally belonged to the Church of England, they became Baptists. My elder brother got engaged to a Roman Catholic girl and joined her church. I remained at our local

Sea Cadets assembled outside St James's Church of Scotland in Worlingham Road.

Postcards were produced showing the interior of St James's Church of Scotland. The site in East Dulwich Road is now occupied by St James's Cloister.

Dulwich Grove Congregational (now United Reformed) Church in East Dulwich Grove was photographed in the early twentieth century.

Congregational church in Dulwich. Sunday dinner times were lively with discussions about each other's churches and beliefs.

Gwendoline Morris in *Go East Young Woman*

Fruit Grew in Orchard

One of our oldest parishioners can remember the Franciscans – who once served our parish – picking fruit in the orchard off Lordship Lane and bringing it to the schoolchildren of St Anthony's. Now where the orchard stood – in Bassano Street – there are houses and the roar of traffic.

Michael Smith in *The Dulwich Catholics 1879-1973*

Star Card Stamped

As a child I attended Sunday School at the Lordship Lane Wesleyan Mission. This was at the corner of Bassano Street opposite where our family lived in Hansler Road.

The person in charge was Mr Thomas Delf. We used to have star cards and, when we attended, the Sunday School teacher put a little star with a rubber stamp on the card. We had to show this to our parents to prove that we had attended.

Margaret Orford (formerly Minnie Pellett) – St Leonards, East Sussex, 2000

CHAPTER 8

Transport

Lordship Lane outside Dulwich Library was busy as passengers boarded a No. 58 tram to Camberwell Green.

Mad Dash for Tram

I had reached the mature age of fourteen years (the school leaving age in 1928), when my mother told me to get a job 'and bring some money into the house'. My parents duly rigged me out in a new fifty-shilling suit ('long-uns' as we called them). Boys always had short trousers up to then. I also had a white shirt and tie, a pair of shoes (instead of boots), a trilby hat and kid-gloves! All set I ventured out.

It was the Easter Holidays for the schools. After a few tries I landed a job as an office boy in the Strand, near the Charing Cross railway station. To start work by 9 a.m. required catching a tram from outside East Dulwich station. This entailed being there before 8 a.m.

A lorry passes the Royal Arsenal Co-operative Society's store in Lordship Lane *c.* 1933. Mrs Ada Brock and her son Derek are seen in the foreground.

Numbers 12 and 78 buses were photographed standing outside The Plough on 2 June 1951.

After a wild dash up the street and round a couple of corners, I joined the crowd at the tram stop (no such thing as a queue then). As the tram came swinging round the bend opposite Elsie Road, there was a wild dash to board it. To have both hands free, I always stuffed my cheese sandwiches and apple into my coat pocket. Those who could held on for dear life until the tram came to a standstill at the stop sign. Depending on whether the conductor was upstairs or downstairs collecting fares, a lucky few would be sailing on towards their destination. Those left behind took their chance on the next wild dash as the tram came swinging round the bend.

On the Embankment at around 6.30 p.m. a similar affair took place when returning to East Dulwich station. My working hours were 9 a.m. to 6 p.m. all week and to 1 p.m. on Saturdays. Wages were the princely sum of fifteen shillings a week!

Leonard R. Moncrieff (Canada), 2001

Went to Greenwich

As a child I used to go with my younger brothers and sister on the tram to Greenwich. We used to take a picnic and go into Greenwich Park and also to the National Maritime Museum. The No. 58 tram used to run all the way from Greenwich to Victoria; I still remember the sound of it rattling along. I also remember East Dulwich for being a terrible place to get transport to travel anywhere. A No. 12 bus went to the West End, but took ages and, even worse, a No. 75 went to Tower Bridge; it was terrible and took for ever. I sometimes went to Peckham Rye Park, for a change, although I didn't like it as much. We used to get an ice cream which was very creamy. One could buy a wafer or a cornet. It seemed very hard but I liked that. My older sister and I often went to swim in the lido on Peckham Rye but it was pretty cold. We also went to Horniman's Museum a lot. I loved it there seeing the huge

A number 58 tram en route to Victoria c. 1950 passes a horse trough where the Goose Green roundabout is today.

A horse bus travels up Barry Road with the spire of Barry Road Wesleyan Church visible above the trees.

A horse and cart travel up Dog Kennel Hill.

Two motor vehicles were snapped going up the hill in Lordship Lane on 4 June 1951.

collection of African artefacts and all those stuffed birds and animals. Across the road was a paddling pond which was great when we had children and took them there in the summer. We also went to Dawson's Hill to play and Horniman's Gardens which also had a paddling pond.

Sheila Davidson, 2001

Buses Disturbed Sleep

After the last tram travelled along Lordship Lane in October 1951, my brother and I suffered disturbed sleep until we became accustomed to the sound of the buses.

Peter Morris, 2001

Few People Owned a Car

Very few people owned cars during the 1940s and there was only one car parked in our road; it belonged to Mr Warelane, my friend's father. The family seldom used it for pleasure, but he needed it to get to Covent Garden vegetable market where he worked. He had to be there very early in the morning before the London Transport was running. I had one ride in the car, when I was taken to join Sylvia and her mother and young sister, Hazel, who were already staying on their grandfather's farm for a part of the summer holiday. I have no idea where the farm was, but to me, it seemed to be a corner of Heaven!

The milkman had a handcart and I do believe he was grateful when we helped him to deliver the bottles (some quart-sized, some pint-sized and some only half-pint). Just about every house had milk from the milkman and it was stored for the day in a

A motor car was the centre of attention in Chesterfield Grove.

cellar or in a bowl of cold water when the weather was warm.

The rag and bone man had a horse and cart and I believe that the coalman also used horsepower in my early days in East Dulwich. We lived in Bassano Street until I was ten years of age, so some things changed over that time. In any case, traffic of any kind was rare, especially in the evenings when work was over for the day. The street was our safe playground for all the years I lived there and we thoroughly enjoyed the games we played together.

Vera Conway, 2001

Passion for Trains Began Early

My baby son, resplendent in his blue woolly pram suit and wearing a pixie hood (the latest fashion), was being taken for a ride in his large cream and brown Silver Cross pram. Everyone stared in envy. Soon several prams like this appeared on the streets.

I would wheel him along to East Dulwich station to see the trains going over the bridge. He would chuckle and wave and seemed thoroughly fascinated. Thirty years later he became a structural engineer to British Railways. His passion is trains of every kind, especially the preservation of old steam trains. He even had part of a steam train in his garden. All this started, I feel sure, from the trains going over the bridge of East Dulwich station.

Grace Smith-Grogan, 2000

Saw Horses pull a Hearse

One of my earliest memories is of sitting up in my 'big' pram in our front room and the Venetian blinds being partially opened so that I could watch a funeral going past with its gleaming black hearse pulled by shiny black horses with black plumes on their heads.

A milkman stands by his horse in Barry Road in 1930.

Later, I had another pram which let down at one end, more like the modern prams or buggies and my mother used to take me to Dulwich Park – quite a pull up Upland Road.

Brenda Pooley, 2001

Washed Father's Car

My father was one of the few people who had a car when I was a child. It was my job to clean it for him for my pocket money. I enjoyed doing that because I used to take the handbrake off and steer it down the road. I don't know if dad knew I did this but if he did, he didn't say anything because he had to walk down the road to drive it back.

We used to be very excited when we saw an aeroplane fly over and would run into the garden in excitement to watch it. It would have come from Croydon Airport which was still functional then. We also saw air raid search lights which continued for a few years after the war.

Sheila Davidson, 2001

Horse Trod on Foot

I had a milk round in East Dulwich, quite a nice area, nice people. I also had this little chestnut mare, she was a good-looking pony but bad tempered, in fact finally she had to be muzzled for our safety.

I will always remember her because one day I was standing by her head entering something in my rounds book. I suppose she thought that she had stood there for long enough and decided to move off.

Off she went, her near fore foot went on my foot, followed immediately by her hind

Frank Russell Staples (1900-76) was a milkman in East Dulwich. The depot he operated from was at No. 148 Lordship Lane. The United Dairies shop was at the corner and the dairy was a few yards away in Melbourne Grove. The stables, which closed in 1940, were in Whateley Road.

Walter Smith sits on his motorcycle outside No. 151 Melbourne Grove soon after the end of the Second World War.

foot; before I could move she had pulled the van over the same foot, front wheel and rear wheel. I was immobile with pain. Of course in those days 'trainers' had not been invented. I had on a solid pair of leather boots tipped and studded so no real damage was done but it made me remember to stand well clear of Ginger in the future.

As time went by I began to wonder why this pony was so bad tempered and I came to the conclusion that it could have been flatulence. If you have never heard a horse 'break wind' you have missed something. It really is a most frightful noise. We can all live with it I know, but sometimes I would be standing by the van talking to a customer and Ginger would decide to relieve herself. I would not know where to put my face and usually the customer would pretend nothing had happened but we'd both know and possibly the customer could not wait to get indoors to laugh. I know I used to giggle. Don't forget this was over fifty years ago,

people looked at things in a different light then.

Frank Staples in *Fifty years in The Milk Game*, 1996

Only Two Cars in Our Road

I was born in Dulwich Hospital in 1935, the youngest of six daughters and grew up in Chesterfield Grove where I still live.

When I was a child our road was very quiet compared with now. I can remember only two cars – one belonged to an up-and-coming young man who owned a Morris Cowley open-top car and caused quite a stir when he took it for a spin each weekend. The other came only occasionally and belonged to Adele Dixon, the famous singer and film star. She would arrive in her chauffeur-driven car and step down in her elegant clothes such as we had never seen and make her way into

Traffic along Lordship Lane approached Eynella Road and Woodwarde Road on Saturday 2 June 1951.

Redgewell's used a motorcycle and sidecar for deliveries.

A No. 58 electric tram goes down Dog Kennel Hill on its way to Blackwall Tunnel.

A No. 37B bus stopped in Melbourne Grove en route to Richmond. Unfortunately No. 37 buses no longer go along Melbourne Grove. Car owners in that road campaigned to have the buses re-routed. This has inconvenienced many bus users especially disabled people.

Deborah Smith stood next to a mini parked outside her father's greengrocer's shop in Lordship Lane in 1967.

A No. 84 tram travels down Dog Kennel Hill en route to the Stuart Road terminus at Peckham Rye while a motorcycle with a sidecar goes up the hill.

A tram approaches the southern end of Grove Vale while a woman pushes a small boy's tricycle.

A No. 56 tram moves up Dog Kennel Hill on its way to Embankment in October 1951.

the house to visit her sister who lived there.

The other traffic was horse-drawn carts bringing bread, milk and coal. There were also the rag and bone man, who rang his bell, the coal cart and dust carts drawn by huge Shire horses.

We all had thick glass plates set into the doorstep on our side of the road as we have cellars which were used to keep coal in. The plate had to be lifted and the front door kept shut while coal was tipped down the hole to the cellar below, as coal dust blew everywhere.

The horses pulling the milk and bread carts came every day and knew exactly where to stop. They also knew where to get a titbit. One of them, I remember, used to mount the pavement and, putting his head over our gate, would nibble the laurel bush while he waited for his carrot.

Gill Harding, 2001

Tram's Brakes Failed

I remember when a tram's brakes failed on Dog Kennel Hill. It ran backwards and pushed a stationary tram along Grove Vale. Fortunately, they did not topple over.

Joseph Hack, 2001

Also Available from Amberley Publishing by John D. Beasley

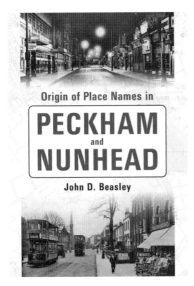

Origin of Place Names in Peckham and Nunhead
ISBN 978 1 84868 224 5   £12.99

Peckham & Nunhead Through Time
ISBN 978 1 84868 290 0   £12.99

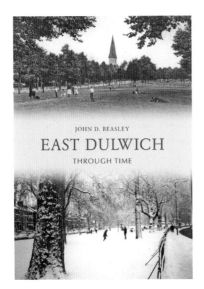

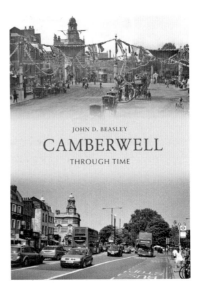

East Dulwich Through Time
ISBN 978 1 84868 550 5   £12.99

Camberwell Through Time
ISBN 978 1 84868 563 5   £14.99